COMBINED OPERATIONS

COMBINED OPERATIONS

The Official Story of the

COMMANDOS

WITH A FOREWORD BY
Vice-Admiral Lord Louis Mountbatten
Chief of Combined Operations

1943

NEW YORK · THE MACMILLAN COMPANY

FOREWORD

London, April 11 (*by Cable*)—This record contains some account of combined operations in general, and of the exploits of the Command which bears that name.

The term "Combined Operations" is vague and does not convey more than a general meaning; but their scope is definite and precise. A combined operation is a landing operation in which, owing to actual or expected opposition, it is essential that the fighting services take part together, in order to strike the enemy with the maximum effect, at the chosen point and at the chosen moment. To help the services to do this a Combined Operations Command was formed, whose primary function is to train officers and men of the Royal Navy and the Royal Marines, the Army and the Royal Air Force in the conduct of amphibious warfare. It is also the task of this Command to plan and execute all kinds of raids, small or large.

Amphibious operations are a complex form of warfare. On the material side they entail technical study, the production of new machines of war, special types of assault craft, both large and small, and the use of these and other new devices. On the human side they demand the creation of sailor-soldiers, soldier-sailors, and airmen-soldiers, who must cooperate with imaginative understanding of each other's methods and problems. The Combined Operations Command is concerned with both of these aspects and with many others.

The Command has its own forces, of which the Commandos and landing-craft crews form a part. But many other units pass through its combined training centres: not only British and Dominion, but also United States troops and those of our other allies—the Fighting French, Norwegians, Czechs, Poles, Dutch, and Belgians. United States Naval, Marine, Army, and Air Corps officers form part of the Combined Operations headquarters, and United States Rangers operate side by side with British Commandos.

We cannot win this war by bombing and blockade alone: it can be won only when our armies have taken physical possession. If we look at the map we find that there is no place where United States or British troops can land to fight the enemy without the probability of severe opposition. They can only be taken there in force by a seaborne expedition with air support. They cannot land unless, in fact, combined operations are carried out. Amphibious warfare, therefore, will play an even greater part in the coming year than it has in the past.

The story of this series of operations has been accurately set down, but it is not complete since, for security reasons, some of our most successful raids cannot yet be mentioned at all, whilst some details of others must remain untold until the war is won.

Louis Mountbatten

PREFACE

This record contains some account of combined operations in general and also of the exploits of the Command bearing that name. Its growth, considerable in 1942, will be still greater in 1943. The story is not complete. Much must remain unsaid, for the war is not yet won and everything cannot therefore be told while there are enemies as well as friends to read it. When it was decided to write the story, the Chief of Combined Operations gave but one order:—"Bearing considerations of security in mind, see to it that the account is accurate and truthful." That order has been obeyed.

The term "combined operations" is vague and does not convey more than a general meaning. Yet their scope is precise and definite.

A combined operation is one in which two or more of the Fighting Services co-operate in order to strike the enemy with the maximum of effect at a chosen place and a chosen moment.

With this end in view, a Combined Operations Command was formed, whose personnel consists of officers and other ranks of the three Fighting Services. Its primary function is to provide training for amphibious warfare, which comprises all kinds of offensive action from small raids to large assault landings. It is also the task of this Command to plan and execute raids on the coasts of the enemy.

Amphibious warfare is a complicated business and has many aspects. On the material side new machines of war, special types of craft, both large and small, to be used for the assault, and other devices for the discomfiture of the enemy, must be studied and produced. On the human side, such warfare necessitates the closest spirit of co-operation in all who wage it.

The Combined Operations Command is concerned with both these aspects and with many others. It produces the craft and the weapons; but above and beyond all else it seeks to foster the spirit of co-operation in all fighting men, united as they are by the danger and glory of their calling. In so doing it is creating in its Combined Training Centres

sailor-soldiers, soldier-sailors, airmen-soldiers, who have a complete understanding of each other's methods and problems.

The Combined Operations Command has its own troops, of which
the Commandos form a part. But many other troops pass through its
hands; not only British and Dominion but also American troops, and
those of other Allies—the Czechs, the Poles, the Norwegians, the Dutch,
the Belgians, the Fighting French—all of them from the array of the
United Nations.

Here is set down the story of a series of operations of which the end
is not yet. In some of them, the Combined Operations Command did
not play the chief part, but served as one of the component elements
involved. Whether these operations failed or succeeded has not been
taken into account. They are presented as they happened. The motto of
those who carried them out and who will play the leading part in those
to come is the motto of the Combined Operations Command—"United
we conquer."

CONTENTS

ILLUSTRATIONS

MAPS

* These maps, in half tone, will be found in the groups of pictures facing the page stated.

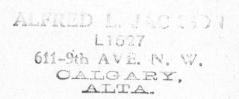

COMBINED OPERATIONS

1. . . . TO BE KNOWN AS COMMANDOS

A little before dawn on the 27th December, 1941, a force of His Majesty's ships was moving through the calm waters of a Norwegian fjord. In the van was a 6-inch cruiser. On her bridge stood a Rear-Admiral and a Brigadier. Astern of her followed destroyers covering two infantry landing ships. The landing craft these carried were being rapidly and silently entered by two Commandos of a Special Service Brigade. A few minutes passed and there came to ears straining to hear it the sound of aircraft engines. Through the thick darkness overhead Hampden bombers of the Royal Air Force swept by. They were not out of earshot before the men in the ships saw coloured lights thrusting vehemently against the sky in a confused and fiery pattern, constantly changed and renewed, and heard above the din of gunfire the duller, louder sound of exploding bombs. The assault on the Island of Maaloy and the town of South Vaagso off the coast of Norway had begun.

It was a combined operation in which officers and men of all three Services took part, and it is the purpose of this narrative to give some account of the conduct of such operations in this present war.

Combined operations are no new development in our history. They are the inevitable consequence of sea power. We were already familiar with them in the sixteenth century when Spain was the adversary. Drake in the West Indies in 1585, Essex and Howard at Cadiz in 1596, showed how a combination of sea and land forces could inflict great hurt on the enemy. It was a lesson once learnt that has never been forgotten, though it has sometimes been badly applied. Against the failure of the expeditions to Walcheren in 1809 and to Gallipoli in 1915 can be set the capture of Gibraltar by George of Hesse-Darmstadt, Rooke and Byng in July 1704, of Quebec by Wolfe and Saunders in September 1759, and of Cape Town by Craig, Clarke and Elphinstone in September 1795. These "conjunct expeditions," to give them their eighteenth-century name, achieved permanent results. Others, such as the burning of eighty French sail in St. Malo in 1758 by a grandson of the great Duke of Marlborough, were

raids designed to inflict loss in men, ships and stores on the enemy. It is
into this latter class that all the combined operations conducted against
the Germans fell until 8th November, 1942, when an army of the United
Nations, supported by a United Nations' fleet and air force, landed in
French North Africa, and by so doing changed the whole course of this
war. Up to then, no more had been attempted than a series of raids in
varying strength carried out on the coasts of countries as far apart as
Norway and Libya.

They began immediately after the fall of France, when the British
Empire found itself fighting almost alone against enemies who held all
the coasts of Western Europe save those of Portugal and Spain, who were
established in North Africa and Abyssinia, who were soon to make
themselves masters of Yugoslavia, Greece and Crete, and whose inten-
tions towards Syria could not even be described as doubtful. Old ambi-
tions, *"non sufficit Orbis,"* that outworn boast which had seemed so
proud to Philip of Spain, which had swelled the heart of King Louis and
led Napoleon through Moscow and the blazing streets of Leipzig to
Waterloo, stirred again in the mean minds of an Austrian paper-hanger
and an Italian stone-mason. In the early autumn of 1940, it must have
seemed to Hitler and Mussolini that, of a truth, the world would not
suffice. Indeed, the first made no secret of his designs—after the British
Empire, Russia; after Russia, the United States; and the second was
ready to follow provided his partner did the fighting. There was a
change of programme as that lovely autumn gave place to an unyielding
winter and the Battle of Britain ended in defeat, not for the Royal Air
Force but for the German Luftwaffe. The order of the victims was
altered, and Russia was placed first on the list. Thus was time given to
us at what was, perhaps, the most critical moment of our history, to
place ourselves in a state and posture not only of defence but gradually
of attack.

The first beginnings could hardly have been more modest, a few raids
by a few men on a few unimportant enemy posts. Then came stronger
raids on more important places, some of them thousands of miles from
England. In these, heavier ships of the Royal Navy and aircraft of the
Royal Air Force played their parts. On 19th August, 1942, came a raid
on Dieppe in which tanks were put ashore and the number of troops
(mostly Canadian) and aircraft employed was far greater than in any
previous operation. Eighty days later the invasion of French North
Africa began, "the greatest combined operation of all time" with the

possible exception of that mounted by the Persian Xerxes—and Herodotus was not very good at figures—some twenty-three centuries earlier and a few hundreds of miles further eastward in the same Mediterranean area. Thus is the process of passing from defence to attack and of building up that attack continuing to develop. One day it will reach its peak.

The Independent Companies

The first troops specifically chosen for raiding were the Independent Companies. They were raised in a hurry to meet the need for offensive operations against the enemy in Norway, and were all volunteers taken from every regiment in the British Army and placed under specially selected officers. Events moved fast—faster than their training programme. Half the companies, under the command of Brigadier C. Gubbins, M.C., soon found themselves in Norway fighting side by side with units of the Regular Army, notably the Scots and Irish Guards, until their final withdrawal from Norway. Their exploits and adventures form part of the Norwegian campaign and will be told when its story is written. Through force of circumstances they did not perform the duties for which they had been brought into being. They did not raid the enemy in the full sense of the word, but fought with him in a more regular manner, and in so doing gave a very good account of themselves. On returning to the British Isles they were established in Scotland and Northern Ireland, where they continued their interrupted training, being shortly afterwards transformed from Independent Companies into Special Service Battalions.

In the meantime the other half of the Independent Companies were still in England fitting themselves for their future task. In May the Norwegian campaign gave place to that of Holland, Flanders and France. Its tragic ending six weeks later found those three countries laid at the proud foot of the conqueror and our own armies back from Dunkirk in good heart but woefully short of weapons and munitions of war. Their survival depended on the avoidance of a straight fight until these were once more in their hands.

The Germans hesitated to embark on the hazardous enterprise of an invasion at least until they had won the mastery of the air. This being denied to them by the valour and skill of Fighter Command, they made no attempt to assault the British Isles otherwise than by bombing attacks carried out under the cover of darkness. A lull in land fighting ensued, during which the main armies of both sides were no longer in contact. Here, therefore, was an opportunity to engage in a kind of amphibious guerrilla warfare to which the British were, by temperament and tradition, peculiarly suited. The national love for the sea could be combined with the national love of the chase; and in this case the quarry would be "the brutish German infantry" now strung out from Narvik to Bordeaux to guard the stolen coasts of Europe and to oppress the peoples they had conquered. The Royal Navy would convey bands of trained soldiers up and down the length of those coasts to demonstrate on small bodies of the enemy that offensive spirit which their less fortunate comrades were, for the moment, unable by force of circumstances to display against his main forces.

This idea commended itself to the Prime Minister and to Sir John Dill, then Chief of the Imperial General Staff, and about a week after the evacuation of Dunkirk, Lieutenant-Colonel D. W. Clarke, Royal Artillery, of that Staff was ordered to prepare a scheme. He was a most experienced officer, with great knowledge of guerrilla warfare gained from service in Palestine at the time of the Arab rebellion. He set to work and in a few days produced the outline of a scheme which had been long in his mind. The men for this type of irregular warfare should, he suggested, be formed into units to be known as Commandos —a name which, he thought, suggested exactly what was wanted. Nor was the historical parallel far-fetched. After the victories of Roberts and Kitchener had scattered the Boer army, the guerrilla tactics of its individual units (which were styled "Commandos") had, for many months, prevented decisive victory from crowning the efforts of forces vastly superior in numbers and arms. Lieutenant-Colonel Clarke had, himself, seen the like feat repeated in Palestine by Arab bands against a whole army corps of regular troops.

His ideas were accepted; so also, with some hesitation, was the name Commando. Two considerations were clear from the outset. First, the Commandos were formed because at that time, June 1940, there was no existing unit of the British Army which could be made available for raiding operations. That is the bald truth. So serious was our situation that not one battalion for many months to come could be spared from the paramount task of organising the defence of the British Isles against invasion. Secondly, the most stringent economy in weapons had to be exercised. All that the factories, working night and day, were able to produce was inevitably earmarked for the main Army. Only a few weapons of modern design were at the disposal of the troops engaged in raiding; or, to put it more exactly, the number of these troops depended on the number of weapons available. So short indeed was the supply of arms at that time that the Commandos had not enough with which to train, and only drew their full complement of such weapons as tommy guns when about to set out on a raid. On their return, the arms went back to a central store.

The Independent Companies had been formed, and special training was given to them in order that they might be available as a force to supplement the Royal Marines, in whom reposes the tradition of amphibious warfare. Such a course was necessary, for the rapidly growing strength of the Royal Navy imposed a considerable strain on the resources in men of the Royal Marines, most of whom at the outbreak of war went to sea in His Majesty's ships and have remained at sea ever since. The Independent Companies were designed to be complete units in themselves, and to be contained in a ship which was to be their home and their floating base. They could thus be moved almost anywhere at very short notice and in a comparatively short time. They were trained to dispense with the normal methods of supply. They were not to depend on the Quartermaster, but were to be, as far as possible, self-contained.

When the Independent Companies gave place to the Special Service Battalions which in their turn were transformed into the Commandos, the original conception of their tactical use was preserved. The Commando or Special Service Troops were to be amphibious. This meant, first and foremost, that they must learn to co-operate with the Royal Navy. Schools for this purpose were established in various convenient places on the coasts of Great Britain so that the men might become familiar with the ways of life, the customs, the habits and the outlook of sailors. These Combined Training Centres were to be, and became, of great importance. They will be referred to again in the next chapter.

Jack and John Go Out Together

To get in and out of a small boat in all kinds of weather, to swim— if necessary in full equipment with firearms held above the water, to be familiar with all the portable weapons of the soldier from the rifle and the tommy gun to the three-inch mortar and the anti-tank rifle, to be able to carry and use high explosives, to hunt tanks and their crews— here are some of the things that the Commando soldier must learn. To do so, however, is only to become proficient in the use of the tools of his trade of war. He must do more than this; he must master his mind as well as his body and become not only a specially trained soldier but a trained individual soldier. In other words, self-reliance and self-confidence form an integral, a vital part of his mental and moral make-up. To achieve these mutually dependent qualities the men, on entering the depot, are treated as far as possible as individuals. They are required to do everything for themselves. It is not for them to await orders from their officer or their N.C.O. They must do the sensible, obvious thing just because it is the sensible, obvious thing.

In so doing they are developing a way of life first taught them when they joined the British Army as recruits, for nearly all of them came to the Commandos having already passed through the rigorous modern training undergone by our Army. Upon this essential and solid foundation the specialised Commando training with its emphasis on individual initiative is superimposed. To give an example. A Troop—the sub-units of a Commando are known as Troops—will come off parade at, say, 3 p.m. and is then told that the next parade will be at 6 a.m. on the following morning at a place 60, 70, sometimes 100 miles away. How each Commando soldier gets to that place is his own affair. The difficulties he may encounter, the shifts to which he may be put to carry out this order do not matter. What does matter is that he be at the appointed place at the appointed time.

Self-confidence springs from the possession of confidence in those appointed to lead. At the depot the embryo Commando soldier soon discovers that his instructors do exactly what he does, only always a little better, however hard he may strive. The old principle of teaching by example bears ripe and rapid fruit.

He is also expected to use his individualism for the common good. If he has a suggestion to make concerning, for example, the best way of carrying one of his weapons, or for moving silently through thick country, he is encouraged to put it forward at once. All ideas are considered on their merits and, if found useful, adopted.

Finally, the young Commando soldier is taught to appreciate to the full the meaning and value of friendship in war. He is encouraged to do everything with a friend and to regard himself as being one of a team of two. Jack always falls in beside John. If Jack is a Bren gunner or an anti-tank rifleman, John is his number two and handles the magazines. When scouts are sent to front or flank, Jack and John go out together. Their team work is vital to the safety and success of the troop moving through enemy country. If Jack is on cookhouse fatigue, John bears a hand. One of the assault courses over which recruits are sent when under training is called "Me and My Pal." It means just what it says. Its obstacles—and they are tough and numerous—have to be overcome together in anticipation of those which will be met and vanquished together on the field of battle. Friendship between two men engaged in the business of war is as old as war itself. Achilles and Patroclus, David and Jonathan, Roland and Oliver, the names change; the spirit remains. Those who train the Commandos have recognised its worth; they foster and cherish it so that the officers who take them into action may know that their men will fight, not with steel only, but with strong united hearts.

The physical conditions of Commando training are strenuous, but well within the endurance of young men all of whom have passed a severe medical test. They march many miles over all kinds of country; they swim rivers or cross them on bridges made of toggle ropes (a toggle rope is a length of cord with a wooden handle at one end and a loop at the other—and is carried by every man). They go over specially-prepared assault courses where only live ammunition and live bombs are used. They climb cliffs; they do physical exercises in parties of eight together bearing a log eight inches thick on their shoulders. When out on a scheme which may last for 18 hours or more, they cook their own food. In camp, they live in tents or huts which they are taught to maintain in a condition of clean smartness rivalling that of the Guards, and their drill, under Guards instructors, is of the same high standard.

Thus, when they reach their Commando Units they are already hard men, physically and morally, able to perform considerable feats of endurance. They have need to be so, for the men they join are harder. One troop in training once marched in fighting order 63 miles in 23 hours and 10 minutes, covering the first 33 miles in eight hours dead. Another in field service order carrying five days' supply of all they needed, marched 130 miles in five days, covering the first 42 of these in 19 hours. Such marches are the rule, not the exception.

When not engaged in active operations the Commandos continue their training. They live, for the most part, in billets and receive no extra pay, but are allowed 6s. 8d. a day with which to keep themselves. In the maintenance of discipline, petty punishments are as far as possible avoided. They have not been abolished altogether, but they are infrequent and the necessity for their infliction does not often arise. The man who commits too many small crimes suffers the final penalty: he leaves his Commando. To judge from some of the letters written by men who have so left and who have asked in vain for a second chance—this is a hard service and second chances are not given—their feelings are akin to those of Adam after his encounter with the Angel bearing the flaming sword.

2. TRAINING FOR ATTACK

Special Service Troops are not the only contingent of the Army who raid the enemy. Many units, American as well as British and Dominion, notably those who took part in the operations against French North Africa, have passed through the Combined Training Centres; many more will do so. Those so trained—and already they number many thousands—will form part of the spearhead of the great offensive when it begins.

One of the first objects of the instruction given at these centres is to make sure that officers and men of the Army become familiar with the way of life pursued by officers and men of the Navy. Thus it is arranged that both live in close contact with each other, sharing the same quarters, eating in the same mess and sleeping in the same conditions. The life of the soldiers immediately takes on a strong naval flavour; they learn to find their way about a ship, to pull a cutter, to enter and leave a small boat, and many other naval matters. Their interest is quickly stimulated; their outlook and their speech begin to change; their minds become filled with naval expressions, naval oaths, and naval slang; they begin to grasp, a little vaguely at first but with swiftly increasing understanding, the meaning of a tradition which has endured for as many centuries as their own. The pride of both Services turns to mutual esteem and therefore to mutual advantage.

A great and successful effort is being made at these centres to achieve a real understanding between the Army and the Navy. The cheers which, one summer day in 1942, greeted the victory of a crew of sergeants and other ranks belonging to the Duke of Wellington's Regiment in a cutter race against a crew of naval ratings, might have caused a superficial observer to imagine that what he was watching was a meeting of a Mutual Admiration Society. He would have been very wrong. Such an understanding, of which this was a small manifestation, shows the existence, not only of good feeling but of the conviction that a task common to both must be carried through by methods each can use and understand. On the 19th August, 1942, a sergeant brought back from Dieppe to England an assault landing craft whose entire naval crew had been killed or grievously wounded. He navigated her by means of an Army compass, since that with which the boat was fitted had been damaged. Such a feat, performed in the ordinary course of duty, is a vindication, if any be needed, of the methods used at these centres.

It is not necessary to enter into details of the training; to do so would be to give information which the enemy would be glad to possess. It must suffice that it is comprehensive, vigorous, and designed to make the fullest and most intelligent use of that spirit of attack which is the secret of the warrior. The Commandos undergo such training in order to fit them for raiding, the purpose for which they were called into being. The armed forces of the United Nations in their thousands are undergoing it so that they may deliver, when the time comes, a sustained and victorious onslaught upon our fierce, our mortal foe.

As with the soldiers, so with the sailors. They are trained to handle the strange diversity of craft used to put the army ashore, take it off after a raid and keep it supplied when on shore. These craft are of curious and unexpected shape. Some of them, such as the assault landing and the tank landing craft, look like oblong floating boxes of steel, and bear as much resemblance to the ordinary conception of a boat as a tank does to a motor car. They are the remote offspring of the "River Clyde," which represented at Gallipoli in 1915 the first attempt to give some protection to troops landing on beaches swept by the fire of the enemy.

The Craft and the Crews

The Combined Operations Development Centre at Portsmouth, formed in 1936, produced the first specially-designed armoured landing craft. It carried thirty-six men in addition to a naval crew, and drew only nine inches forward. It was self-propelled, proof against rifle and machine-gun fire, and could be carried at the davits of a merchant ship. The factors governing the design of such craft, whether they are to land troops, tanks, vehicles or artillery, correspond to the requirements for success. These are—speed in getting on to the beaches, protection during the process, ability to put troops ashore on as wide a front as possible, the provision of covering fire during the assault and the maintenance of supplies in its early stages. Craft such as these are far from handy; their blunt bows, which open to release down hinged ramps, men, tanks or vehicles, are ill fitted to plough through a head sea, and their flat bottoms make them poor sea boats in rough or even choppy water. They are of several kinds and dimensions, and are powered mostly by American engines.

In contrast to the blunt-nosed assault craft, there is the personnel landing craft of American construction. It is a motor vessel, fast and seaworthy; but it is of small size and has no armour. It is used mostly at night.

Landing craft are carried by infantry landing ships, originally known as assault ships, of which many were employed in the days of peace in the less hazardous task of carrying travellers on their lawful occasions to ports all over the world. When on an operation they are escorted by various types of motor gunboat, motor torpedo boat and motor launch. These are fast—some of them very fast—and they make up what are known as our Light Coastal Forces. Their exploits have been described in many Admiralty communiqués. Behind them are the destroyers detailed to act as covering forces, if necessary; and behind these, ultimately, is the Home Fleet.

The officers and men who man the landing craft, the gunboats and launches are, for a great part, enlisted for the duration of hostilities only —the H.O.s as they are known in the Royal Navy. It is in the handling of such craft that the experience of the Merchant Navy officer, now an officer with the Royal Naval Reserve, and of the peacetime yachtsman, now a member of the Royal Naval Volunteer Reserve, is of the greatest value. There is something, perhaps much, to be said in wartime for the enthusiastic amateur who carries out his duties under the guidance and command of regular officers of the Royal Navy. Such men know the waters round these islands and those that wash the western coasts of Holland, Belgium and France as few know them, and when it comes to putting ashore a few dozen men of a Commando in a quiet Breton cove or several battalions of assault-trained infantry on half a dozen scattered beaches, that knowledge tells.

When not on patrol or engaged in an operation, they live in shore establishments run on strictly naval lines. When a car arrives, for instance, to take someone away, the naval sentry will report that it is "alongside"; the bedrooms are "cabins"; the living room "the wardroom"; the terrace fronting the estuary, where strong-winged duck fly in season above the opalescent mud, is the "quarter deck." Here they train as strenuously as does the army, and here, too, their craft are maintained and repaired. Much of this, and all the office work, is done by the members of the Women's Royal Naval Service—the Wrens. Ratings belonging to this famous corps also handle picket boats and other small harbour craft and by so doing, have earned the nickname "Water Hens."

The training undergone is designed to overcome the problems of approaching the shore, landing on it, remaining off it within instant call and re-embarking troops from it. Much of it appears highly unorthodox. Men who, for years, have regarded running a ship aground as the first, last and most perfect example of professional incompetence, now spend their days doing little else. How to beach, when to beach, how long to remain aground, how best to use a kedge for getting off, how to avoid the disaster of stripping a propeller—these are some of the problems they learn to master. They need no Canute to tell them that the tide never stands still. If it is going out, then the landing craft must be continually eased down the beach towards deeper water or she will become stranded. If the tide is coming in, she must be driven with it up the beach or a cross wind may catch her and put her bows about.

"The business of keeping a ship beached but not stranded, shuffling it on its belly up and down the shore while it is being loaded or unloaded, possibly under fire, is no game for any but the trained." It is here that the man joined for war service only is especially suitable. To one accustomed to years of service in a destroyer, a cruiser or a battleship, this art of beaching—for it is an art—seems sometimes a little peculiar; but the man who a few months before was a foreman, a clerk or a salesman, has never known any other form of naval existence and does not therefore have to overcome the habits of half a lifetime. "The good thing about this job," says one of them, "is that we all know we are doing something that has never been done before."

The living accommodation on these craft is very cramped, even in the larger types of motor gunboats. When the army is on board there is very little room indeed. The captain of a gunboat once tried to reach his quarters. He returned baffled to his bridge and was heard to mutter, "There are fifty soldiers frying bacon in my wardroom." Close co-operation between the services is of the body as well as of the mind.

One of the most important and dangerous duties is that performed by the Beachmaster and his opposite number, the Military Landing Officer. They work as a team and their task is to control the beaches with the help of Assistant Beachmasters and Unit Landing Officers. They must see that the beach is clearly marked so that craft moving in later will not mistake it; they must discover and mark the best exits from it towards the country behind; they must attend to craft coming ashore, to the hauling-away of vehicles which may have become stuck in the sand or shingle and to the re-floating of craft aground. For this and other purposes the Bulldozer, a small tracked vehicle with a movable steel shovel in front of it and tremendous pushing power, is invaluable. It is the Beachmasters who call in the boats to take off the men returning from a raid; while on the beaches they are, indeed, at once the constable on point duty and the foreman in charge of the delivery van.

Air Co-operation and Airborne Assault

The training of the Royal Air Force in combined operations is proceeding side by side with that of the other two services. Its most obvious task is to provide in daylight air cover for the craft carrying the troops and for the naval forces protecting them, and close support during the attack. Co-operation with the Army, which in this war began with the campaign in Flanders, is the special business of Army Co-operation Command. More and more squadrons are coming into service with it, some of which shared in the great air victory over Dieppe.

Just as the Royal Navy puts the infantry ashore in small boats, so does the Royal Air Force take parachute or glider-borne troops to their objectives. The main difference between the two operations lies in the training. Airborne troops have the harder task. They jump, not from the ramp of an assault landing craft, but from the belly of an aircraft. For this they require special training and equipment. After a preliminary period of jumping from a platform and a captive balloon, they practise dropping from an aircraft, first in "slow" then in "quick" pairs, until they are proficient enough to drop in "sticks." This they do through a hole in the floor of the fuselage above which are two lights—a red switched on when the pilot is beginning his run-in to the dropping zone and a green indicating that the moment to jump has arrived. Each man in turn slips in a sitting position from the edge of the hole. His parachute is on his back carried in a bag divided into two sections. He first falls the length of his "strop", a cord of which one end is firmly attached to the aircraft, the other being joined to a length of cord known as his "static line." This is housed in the top half of the bag and on becoming taut pulls out the rigging lines which in turn pull out the canopy. The whole process takes between two and three seconds.

"On falling through the hole your legs are immediately blown sidewards by the slip stream and you find yourself parallel to the ground. A moment later there is a nibbling feeling at your shoulders; the canopy has opened; but the jerk is no harder than that made by a fair-sized trout when you hook it. After that, all sensation of falling ends. When near the ground, it is the earth moving up to meet you and not you meeting the earth, which you notice." The landing is no light matter. Only those who have jumped off the roof of a slowly-moving train can have an idea of what it is like. It was troops trained on these lines who seized the North African airfields and formed the spearhead of the First Army.

The pilots of the aircraft carrying the airborne troops must be most exactly trained. They have to drop live bodies, not live bombs; and while a bomb may do much damage even if it does not fall directly on the target, an airborne soldier can effect nothing and will in all probability very swiftly become a casualty unless he is dropped exactly in the right place and in the company of all or most of his comrades. Troops carried in gliders are also trained with the Royal Air Force, whose aircraft tow the gliders and whose fighters afford them the most necessary protection. The pilots belong to the Army but are trained by the Air Force.

Much of the air support given in a combined operation is indirect, in the sense that the aircraft taking part in it may be attacking targets many miles distant from the centre of the raid. Bombers can be, and are, used to prevent the arrival of reinforcements, to break up tank concentrations, and generally to harass the enemy striving to rush troops and aircraft to the defence of a threatened position.

In the raid on Vaagso on the 27th September, 1941, the enemy airfield at Herdla, a hundred miles distant, was put out of action at the critical moment by a perfectly-timed bombing attack. German bombers hastening from Holland to bomb the raiding force attacking Dieppe on the 19th August, 1942, were intercepted by our fighters thirty miles or more to the north over the mouth of the Somme, while the main German fighter airfield, at Abbeville, was knocked out for the day by American Flying Fortresses.

Masters of a New Technique

Raids, large and small, are the responsibility of the Chief of Combined Operations, who plans them with the aid of a small expert staff, nearly all of whom have had practical experience in this form of warfare, and who not infrequently take an active part in the operation which they themselves have helped to plan. Their growing knowledge and experience are at the disposal at all times of those responsible for the general direction of the war, and have been put to good use. General Eisenhower, for example, has stated that in the successful operations on the north coast of Africa "much was owed to the assistance received from, and the work done by 'Combined Operations' in the preparatory and assault stages." These planners are becoming masters of a new technique. They belong to all three Services, and each has special knowledge of his own Service. They acquire knowledge of the other two by working closely and constantly together and discussing every problem as it arises. After every raid the lessons learnt are carefully noted and discussed, so that next time a particular mistake may be avoided, a successful method of attack exploited.

To aid them they have at their disposal a large and ever-increasing volume of intelligence collected from many sources at the risk of many lives, and covering everything that a raider, and presently an invader, ought to know. For the raid on Dieppe, for instance, a Confidential Book of 48 quarto pages with a compendium of maps and plans displaying in the greatest detail the enemy's defences, known or suspected, was prepared, printed and distributed to those concerned. Without intelligence of this kind no raid, whatever its size, has much chance of success. Accurate knowledge of the enemy, of his methods of defence and counter-attack, of his weapons and his morale is as indispensable as is the rifle or the grenade. On good intelligence depend both the plans and their execution. The modern soldier is no longer sent into battle with—as so often happened in the last war—only a vague, general idea of what his task is to be. He is carefully and accurately briefed, and it is intelligence which provides the material for such briefing.

So much, then, for general considerations. It is time to set down—in part only, for much must still remain secret—the story of raiding from the modest beginning on the coast of France in June 1940, to the attack on Morocco and Algiers which resulted in the occupation of those countries, and is in itself but a prelude to that final assault by which victory will be achieved.

3. THE STEEL HAND FROM THE SEA

Shortly before midnight on the 2nd September, 1942, Ober Maat (Chief Mate) Munte, who had once been a stoker in the German Navy, was seated in his office in the Casquet lighthouse seized by his master when the Channel Islands were occupied in July 1940. He was busy making up returns—an occupation well fitted to his rank and experience. A slight noise—it may have been the click of the door as it closed softly—caused him to turn in his chair. Leaning against the door were two men with black faces, wearing crumpled khaki uniforms, somewhat damp round the ankles. Two Colt automatics, negligently poised, were in their hands. He got slowly to his feet and passed a hand across his eyes, but, when he dropped it, the figures by the doorway were still there. Chief Mate Munte began to sway and, as one of the Special Service men stepped forward, collapsed fainting with terror on the floor. To bring him round, the two black-faced men slapped his cheeks, and a short while afterwards he was in a small boat bobbing uneasily in the treacherous waters that surge about the lighthouse he had failed to guard. By then he was in the company of the six men who formed his command. They were the wireless operators and the guard of the lighthouse. Those who had not been on watch were still in their pyjamas and were wearing hair nets, which at first caused the commander of the raiding party to mistake one of them for a woman. By four o'clock in the morning, after a stormy passage, the Germans found themselves prisoners of war in England.

Raids such as this take place frequently on the coast of German-occupied Europe. Not much is said about them either by ourselves or by the enemy. Sometimes however, perhaps when a particularly galling barb has been implanted in his hide, he cries out. Then something can be said of the manner of its planting. These small raids began in June 1940.

On the 12th of that month Lieutenant-General Sir Alan Bourne, K.C.B., D.S.O., Adjutant-General of the Royal Marines, was placed by the Prime Minister in charge of raiding operations with Brigadier (then

ATTACKS ON THE
COASTS OF EUROPE

To SPITZBERGEN

NARVIK

LOFOTEN IS

GLOMFJORD

A R C T I C   C I R C L E

ICELAND

TRONDHJEM

VAAGSÖ

HERDLA
BERGEN
LILLEBÖ

STAVANGER

STOCKHOLM

OSLO

Scapa Flow

N O R T H

S E A

EDINBURGH

COPENHAGEN

BELFAST

DUBLIN

Heligoland
Bight
Frisian Is.

HAMBURG

BERLIN

AMSTERDAM

LONDON

ZEEBRUGGE

CAP D'ALPRECH
BRUSSELS

PRAGUE

N

GUERNSEY

CASQUET
DIEPPE
BRUNEVAL

LE HAVRE

USHANT
BREST

LORIENT

ST NAZAIRE

PARIS

BERNE

O
C
E
A
N

A
T
L
A
N
T
I
C

LA PALLICE

BORDEAUX

MILES 50 0   200   400

KILOMETRES 0   200   400   600

Lieutenant-Colonel) A. H. Hornby, M.C., Royal Artillery, as his Chief of Staff. A small headquarters was formed, and housed by the Admiralty which had a vacant set of offices to spare. They were to plan and organise raids, their proposals being first submitted through the Joint Planning Committee of the three Services to the Chiefs of Staff. For the execution of these plans Lieutenant-Colonel Clarke, whose connection with the Special Service troops has been mentioned in Chapter I, set about finding suitable men from the volunteers composing the Independent Companies, while Captain Garnons-Williams, D.S.C., R.N., began to get together such small craft as could be found and the officers and men to man them. The craft were an odd collection, mostly private motorboats, some of which in peacetime had sailed the quiet waters of the Hamble or the Norfolk Broads. Their design and sea-going qualities were as varied as the reliability of their engines. The assault landing craft, of which the prototype had appeared in 1936, were not yet available.

The officers were mostly amateurs in the sense that very few belonged to the Royal Navy. Some came from the Royal Naval Reserve, but most belonged to the Royal Naval Volunteer Reserve. Among them were many enthusiastic and capable yachtsmen. The hands were mostly fishermen—capable, willing, but at first somewhat surprised at naval discipline. It is related of one of them that during his daily bathe in the river on which the depot was situated, he met in mid-stream his captain, who was being put across in a dinghy. The following dialogue was overheard by a stricken first lieutenant on the bank.

> *The Sailor:* Oi!
> *The Captain* (turned his head but did not speak).
> *The Sailor:* You going over there?
> *The Captain:* (austerely) Yes.
> *The Sailor:* Give us a tow, mate.

No time was lost. By the 15th June, 1940, a depot, first a converted yacht but soon other quarters, on shore had been established on the south coast of England and the training of both Services in amphibious warfare began. Intense energy prevailed from the start, and on the night of 23rd/24th June the first raid took place.

It was a reconnaissance of the French Coast between Cap d'Alprech near Boulogne, and the Pointe du Hautbanc near Berck. Two hundred men were to be landed in six (subsequently changed to four) parties, to discover the nature of the German defences, and bring back prisoners.

The landings were, if possible, to take place at the same time in order to confuse the enemy. The Senior Naval Officer was Lieutenant-Commander J. W. F. Milner-Gibson, R.N., who had been ashore on the coast of France nine times in the three weeks preceding the operation in order to spy out the land. The troops were under the command of Major R. J. F. Todd, Argyll and Sutherland Highlanders. Lieutenant-Colonel Clarke also went on the raid but was ordered not to land.

The party sailed from three southern ports. Various changes in the dispositions had to be made, for some of the craft proved too slow and others developed defects on passage from the depot to the ports of sailing. At the last moment, fast light motor boats became available and the men were embarked upon them, but there was room only for 120 in all. The remainder had to be left behind. The weather was favourable. A light breeze was blowing from the north-east; the sea was calm, the sky cloudy. There was also some haze interspersed with patches of fog. The three groups of the Force sailed before dark to keep a rendezvous some ten miles out in the Channel. Having done so, they went on in company and then split up once more and made off for their respective landing places. They met with varying fortunes. Two boats landed their troops on a waste of sand dunes where no living being was encountered. German aircraft flew constantly over their heads but did not see them. Another boat approached the coast near Boulogne. When close in, the men on board her perceived that they were in the midst of an enemy seaplane anchorage. To land undetected was obviously impossible. It was decided to wreck one of the seaplanes; but, as the boat moved towards it, the aircraft selected suddenly took off and roared over their heads, missing them by a few feet. The Germans on shore were now on the alert, and since surprise was lost the troops did not land.

The boat carrying Major Todd with Lieutenant-Colonel Clarke made a landfall, and the soldiers moved off into the darkness, making no sound on the soft sand. In accordance with his orders Lieutenant-Colonel Clarke remained with the boat, standing in her bows. About an hour later Major Todd returned, having posted his men a short distance inland. They had met with no Germans; but as he was debating with Lieutenant-Colonel Clarke where next to look for some, five appeared. Major Todd was about to engage them with his tommy gun when the magazine fell off with a clatter. The Germans opened fire and then fled. Lieutenant-Colonel Clarke was hit a glancing blow behind the ear. This was the only casualty sustained throughout the operation and the wound was superficial. Hearing the shots, Major Todd's men returned. "At first I did not know," said Lieutenant-Colonel Clarke, "who they were. They might have been the German patrol. All I could see in the moonlight—for the clouds had by now disappeared—was a number of sinister figures moving slowly and purposefully towards me with out-thrust bayonets. It was only when they were near enough for me to see their blackened faces that I knew them to be our own men. That is one of the main difficulties about raiding at night. It is so hard to tell friend from foe."

Another party had better luck. They made the Plage de Merlimont, four miles south of Le Touquet, and approached a large building surrounded by barbed wire. It was full of the enemy. Two sentries were set upon and killed, but one of them cried out before he died and gave the alarm. It was impossible to rush the house because of the wire, so the attackers lobbed grenades through the windows and then withdrew without loss.

The force reached England in broad daylight, the boats coming home independently. Their reception was mixed. At one port, those on board a boat were refused permission to enter the harbour as no one was sure of their identity. They lay off the boom, covered by the guns on shore, wet through and after a time slightly intoxicated by the contents of two jars of rum which, fortunately for them, were on board. Their troubles did not end when they got on shore, for they were then arrested by the Military Police who took them for deserters. At another port, the companies of the ships in harbour cheered the raiders as they made fast to the jetty. Those cheers were echoed in the Press, which made the most of the laconic communiqué describing the operation. To do so was natural enough, for the raid took place at a time when our fortunes were at a low ebb. In fact, it was no more than a reconnaissance, not even in force, but it achieved its purpose. Not only had information of military value been brought back, but men of the Royal Navy and the Army had together carried out a combined operation against the enemy and had laid that foundation of mutual confidence that was to be of such vital importance later on.

Getting Back from Guernsey

The next raid took place, on Guernsey, on the night of 14th/15th July, 1940. It was carried out by elements of No. 3 Commando under Major (now Lieutenant-Colonel) J. F. Durnford Slater, Royal Artillery, and of No. 11 Independent Company under Major Todd and Captain Goodwin, the Suffolk Regiment. They were taken to the island in two de-stroyers, H.M.S. "Scimitar" and H.M.S. "Saladin," followed by the motor boats which were to put them ashore. One boat, whose compass went wrong, missed Guernsey and visited "a shore with high cliffs and no beaches, believed . . . to be the island of Sark." Another party had difficulties with the motor boats and with H.M.S. "Saladin's" whaler, which was pressed into service but was leaking. They failed to make land but eventually got safely back to England, making the last part of the voyage under the protection of the Royal Air Force.

The third landing party under Lieutenant-Colonel Durnford Slater was more successful. The boats reached the right beach but could not go close in owing to rocks, and the men had to wade ashore up to their waists in water. Their movements up the steep path from the beach were very silent, what few sounds they made being drowned by the noise of Anson aircraft of Coastal Command which flew by arrangement over-head. The Jerbourg peninsula was thoroughly searched, but the barracks, where the enemy was expected to be, were found empty. The re-embarka-tion proved very difficult and slow. One of the two motor boats was badly damaged and neither could get nearer than 50 yards to the beach, on which waves about three feet high were now breaking. Several men were ferried to one of the boats in a small dinghy, but it capsized on its last trip and all the tommy guns with which it was laden were lost, together with one man. The remainder eventually swam out, all save three who were not strong enough swimmers and had to be left behind exhausted. The boats eventually reached the "Scimitar" and all got safely back to England, for part of the time under air escort.

No-Man's Land Is No-Man's Sea

The last two raids described took place in the summer of 1940, and have been followed by many more, particularly during the weeks pre-ceding and following the attack on Dieppe on 19th August, 1942. Some-times their object is, as in the raid on the Casquet lighthouse, to remove prisoners and destroy valuable apparatus; at other times to reconnoitre the coast and test the degree of alertness shown by the enemy.

They take place at night. Small parties of the strength of a troop or less go ashore from assault landing craft on to a beach selected from the study of intelligence reports. They carry out a reconnaissance and return, their time on shore being governed by the tide and the weather, always factors of cardinal importance. The following extracts from the

official reports on two different raids in 1941 illustrate the conditions
under which such small scouting expeditions are carried out. The first
describes the activities of a patrol on shore pressed for time since they
had been delayed on passage to France.

"Crossing the road and turning right-handed the patrol came upon a
shuttered house. A brief examination revealed no occupants. . . . Time
was now running short, it being 0155 hours.* The leading scouts of the
patrol, proceeding up the road for greater speed, reached a bend at the
same time as a German cyclists' patrol travelling in the opposite direction.
Fire was immediately opened upon the Germans with tommy guns at
point-blank range, and it is unlikely that any of them escaped serious
injury. Two bodies were carried back towards the assault landing
craft. . . ."

While the troops are thus engaged the men of the Royal Navy wait
in the landing craft. In one such raid they listened to the sounds of
rifle- and machine-gun fire, soon coming under fire themselves. Presently
footsteps were heard. "The landing party was by now returning—and
by 0215 were all on board. Assault landing craft No. 123 hauled off the
beach on the kedge. . . . It was then realised that something was wrong
in the engine room. Neither telegraph nor voice-pipe was obeyed. I sent
Sub-Lieutenant E. Poole, R.N.V.R., to the engine room, who reported
that the stoker (Stoker Booker) had been killed and one engine was out
of action. He took charge, and in complete darkness got one engine
going. Having cleared the shoal-water I turned the assault landing craft
to seaward. Just at this moment, 0225 approximately, an enemy plane
flew over at a height of 50 feet, dropping flares, and searchlights appeared,
sweeping both from the north and south of my position. I retired at full
speed on one engine, assault landing craft No. 73 in company, and neither
the plane dropping flares nor the searchlights picked us up."

The information obtained by these small-scale operations is very useful.
Such reconnaissance activity may be compared with trench raids of the
last war when, beneath the Very lights, patrols crawled over the wilder-
ness of No-Man's Land in a desolation of shell holes and rusty wire to
obtain that information without which no commander can form a successful plan of attack. Nowadays No-Man's Land is No-Man's Sea—the
uneasy waters of the Channel.

These raids have been going on at intervals throughout the last two-

---

* The Army and the Air Force add the word "hours" after the time mentioned; the
Navy does not. Both use the 24-hour clock.

and-a-half years. The raid on the Casquet lighthouse was but one of many.

A few days later, an operation, small if the numbers taking part in it are considered, but large in its consequences, took place many hundreds of miles to the northward, on the coast of Norway. A number of officers and other ranks from No. 2 Commando and other Army organisations attacked the Glomfjord Hydro-electric Power Station. This is a plant of considerable importance supplying current to the chief aluminium manufacturing plant in Norway, which is situated a few miles away. The party was under the command of Captain G. D. Black, M.C., South Lancashire Regiment, with Captain J. B. J. Houghton, Queen's Own Cameron Highlanders, as second-in-command.

Across the "Black Glacier"

Captain Houghton and a companion reconnoitred the route ahead and returned after four hours, having found a suitable way across the "black glacier." A meal was eaten; the party moved off and bivouacked for the rest of the night near the glacier. The next morning they started up the steep mountain side and were soon on the ice. The toggle ropes they had with them proved useful when it came to crossing a number of crevasses met with in their passage over the glacier. That evening, they were within sight of the pipe-line bridling the mountain torrent which supplied the motive power to the turbines and dynamos of the power house.

After a rest, they pressed on; but the precipitous nature of the way put them into great peril, for they were soon moving along the side of a mountain which at this point fell sheer into a lake. There were many loose stones and boulders on the rough track which led slowly downwards. To dislodge one of these would bring down others and set the whole wild valley roaring. Treading delicately, they descended in silence and darkness, and by dawn they had reached good cover within a short distance of the power station, now clearly visible.

At eight o'clock in the evening they held a conference and Captain Black explained his plan. Two of them, Sergeant Smith and Guardsman Fairclough, the first of the Coldstream, the second of the Grenadier Guards, were detailed to demolish the machinery of the power house. Two others, Lance-Sergeant O'Brien, of the Royal Berkshire Regiment, and Private Makan, of the London Scottish, were to put charges under the pipe-line. Others were to guard the power house while the demolition party was at work. The remainder would form a covering party. The power station is connected with Glomfjord village by a tunnel, and it was near its entrance that Captain Black stationed himself.

Shortly before eleven in the evening, the party went about its appointed tasks. A way was found into the station through one wing, which was being rebuilt. Captain Houghton and a companion crawled under a canvas screen and had got well inside when they caught a glimpse of one of the guards. They dashed at once into the guardroom, held up the guards, and then took them downstairs. Almost immediately afterwards a German was met with and shot.

All this time the demolition party, who had slipped in on the heels of Captain Houghton and his companion, were at work; and presently they reported that the charges were laid. The party then moved off. A few minutes later there were two explosions. A vivid glow was seen through the windows and doors of the power house, which seemed to shake and quiver. Flames shot up, and at that moment the air raid siren sounded in Glomfjord village.

The raiders pressed on and presently halted to wait for those who had been detailed to deal with the pipe-line. A roar, which sent the echoes flying round the lake, told them that here, too, success had been achieved; and presently the pipe-line demolition party arrived with Captain Black, who had stayed behind to cover them. United once more, they all moved off, but soon became involved in a fight with a number of Germans. There were some casualties on both sides.

The destruction wrought was in the highest degree effective. The power station was wrecked, and it is highly improbable that it can be put into proper working order again until the war is ended. This means that the aluminium works in Glomfjord, which had recently been enlarged, will also be idle.

160,000 Tons of Iron Pyrites

The story of one more such raid may be told, though it took place in January, 1943, and is, therefore, strictly speaking, outside the scope of this account. It is, however, a typical example of the kind of enterprise into which the small-scale raids, begun in the summer of 1940, have now developed and for that reason it is included.

On the night of 23rd/24th January, 1943, a number of motor torpedo boats, manned by Norwegians, with Commando soldiers on board, arrived off the south-western coast of Norway. The objective of the troops was an iron pyrites mine situated at Lillebö in the island of Stord, and the second largest of its kind in Norway.

The attackers were divided in two groups. The first was to cover the activities of the second, whose duty it was to destroy the mine. The first group approached the quayside of the small village of Saagvag. Their landing was opposed, but after a brisk fight they cleared the quay, took a number of prisoners and proceeded to establish road blocks and cut telephone wires. While this first party went about their several tasks, the second force had been landed on the other side of Saagvag Bay. Once ashore, they pressed on towards the mine, covering a distance of two miles in 25 minutes, each man of them heavily laden with demolition charges. Arrived at their objective, they at once set about its destruction. The hoisting gear above the mine was blown up and fell down the shaft, the crushing plant, the compressor house, the transformer and a railway shed nearby were blown to pieces. The demolition force then made its way back to the quayside, held by the covering force.

In the meantime, out at sea, the naval covering force of motor torpedo boats had not been idle. One of them, moving round the island, encountered an enemy merchant vessel of about 2,000 tons which she sank by gunfire. She also silenced an enemy gun position on shore, and together with another motor torpedo boat, shelled other enemy positions along the coast.

In the small hours of the morning the troops were re-embarked. Before going on board they got rid of such demolition charges as remained by blowing up a silo at the quayside, the conveyor system, the ore crusher and four enemy gun positions, together with their ammunition. On the way home the small force shot at and hit a Ju.88 which exploded in the air.

Thus at the cost of one N.C.O. killed, and a number of minor casualties, a mine providing the Germans with 160,000 tons of iron pyrites a year was so effectively destroyed as to be out of action for at least twelve months, an enemy merchant ship was sunk and much other damage done.

Such are the hazards of these small raids. They are carried out by resolute and determined men, in whose hearts love of country and love of adventure are happily blended.

4. DESTRUCTION IN THEIR WAKE

By 1941 a change of plan, or rather policy, in the matter of raiding the enemy had taken place. It was felt by then that small-scale raids, though of great value, were not enough. Something larger must be attempted. This took time and the Commandos learnt patience as one of the lessons of their training, for disappointments were frequent. All through the summer and autumn of 1940, training had been steadily progressing. New Combined Operational Training Centres were gradually established, special craft gradually collected. A number of passenger steamers and two train ferries were made over to the Director of Combined Operations, transformed into infantry landing ships and added to the converted liners already in use. A start was made with the recruiting and training of parachute troops.

On 17th July, 1940, Admiral of the Fleet Sir Roger Keyes, G.C.B., K.C.V.O., C.M.G., D.S.O., M.P. (now Baron Keyes of Zeebrugge and Dover), was appointed Director of Combined Operations in place of Lieutenant-General Sir Alan Bourne, of the Royal Marines, who willingly consented to serve as his Second-in-Command. This appointment was made to mark the change in policy from small to larger-scale raids though, for lack of enough ships and trained men, they could not be immediately undertaken.

Before the first of them took place, on the Lofoten Islands, on 4th March, 1941, a combined operation of a new type was undertaken. By the beginning of 1941, a sufficient number of parachute troops had been trained to make a small-scale operation feasible. The target chosen was some 1,800 miles from Great Britain.

In the province of Campagna, which is in the ankle of Italy, there is an aqueduct spanning a small stream, the Tragino. This was the objective chosen, and it was not very easy to find, for it is situated in the wild and desolate country lying to the south-west of Monte Vulture.

Its destruction was a job for men handy with explosives and trained in the art of demolition. It was entrusted to a small party of officers and other ranks of an Airborne Division. Half belonged to the Royal Engineers and the remainder were to act as a covering party. The Senior Officer in charge of the Force was Major T. A. C. Pritchard, and the air arrangements were under the direction of Wing Commander (now Group Captain) Sir Nigel Norman, Bt. The expedition was carefully planned and rehearsed in England under the direction of the late Lieutenant-Colonel J. F. Rock, R.E., and on the 7th February eight Whitleys bearing the parachute troops took off from an airfield in East Anglia on the first stage of their flight. Their destination was Malta, where they arrived on the next day, having been preceded by a Short Sunderland flying boat with maintenance staff and equipment.

Indifferent weather had prevented the taking of photographs of the objective, but, on the 9th February, Flying Officer (now Acting Wing Commander) A. Warburton, D.S.O., D.F.C., piloting a Glen Martin, took good pictures of the target area. They disclosed the existence of two aqueducts about 200 yards apart; that to the east, it was decided, was the one to be destroyed. Having done so, the parachutists were to make their way to a point on the west coast of Italy, and there be taken on board a submarine. Two days were spent in Malta making last-minute preparations, and on the 10th February the eight Whitleys took off in the evening light. Six of them carried the parachute troops and their equipment, and two were loaded with bombs with which to create a diversion. The rendezvous for the Whitleys was Monte Vulture and five of them reached it on time. The sixth, aircraft "J," was late in starting owing to a last-minute defect and did not reach the neighbourhood of the dropping area until 11.15, an hour and a quarter behind time. Unluckily this had on board Captain G. F. K. Daly, R.E., who was to have been in charge of the demolitions. As will be seen, Second Lieutenant G. R. Patterson, R.E., shouldered the responsibility and had to make some risky decisions.

The Main Charge Was Fired

The parachutists dropped from the five aircraft in a good pattern round the target, the man farthest away falling on the pebble bank of the River Ofanto. Conditions were perfect: there was snow on the hillsides above the aqueduct, and bright moonlight. The first party landed at 9.42 p.m. with its officer only 50 yards from the objective. After collecting their weapons and forming up they were ordered to search the farm buildings nearby. These were of the ordinary southern Italian type, low two-storeyed houses, the farmer and his family living in the top storey, while the ground floor was occupied by his beasts.

By this time Major Pritchard and Lieutenant Patterson had come up, but there was no sign of Captain Daly. Patterson at once inspected the aqueduct and found that the three piers supporting the structure were not made of masonry as had been thought, but of reinforced concrete, more difficult to destroy by explosives. Taking a risk, he at once decided to concentrate on the westernmost pier. Though a number of containers had failed to leave the aircraft, he hoped that he would have with him explosives sufficient for the purpose, for in calculating the amount required a large margin had been left.

While Patterson and his sappers were preparing the demolition the other officers and men were disposed as a covering party. A quarter of an hour after midnight the main charges were all laid. There was still some spare explosive, and Lieutenant A. G. Deane-Drummond decided to blow up a small bridge near him which crossed the Ginestra, a tributary of the Tragino. The track running over this bridge had been used in the construction of the objective, and it occurred to him that to destroy it would hinder the work of repair.

Major Pritchard decided to blow the charges at half-past twelve, and a minute before this a single slab of gun-cotton was fired as a warning to the covering party. At half-past twelve the main charge went off and half a minute later the small bridge blew up.

Their task accomplished, the parachutists collected round Major Pritchard. For the journey to the coast he divided them into three independent groups, each under an officer. He and his party set off westwards, and when dawn came hid in a wood for the day. At dusk on the second night they moved out westwards and kept in the fields by a road, skirted a little town, and then made good going along the road for the next four miles. They then struck south-west over the flank of the mountain, but by then it was time to look for a place to lay up for the day. Their map marked a wood above them. They toiled up¡but only found snow as the dawn was breaking. They scrambled up into the snow and hid in a small cave and behind rocks.

Their tracks in the mud and snow led up to their hiding-place. It was not long before a farmer came up, found them, and gave the alarm. Then, from high up the mountain, they watched the comedy of the search parties approaching in the growing light. First came the village dogs, led by three pointers; then the village children, wondering where the dogs were going; then the women, racing after the children to bring them back, followed by the men who had gone out to protect their womenfolk. Behind these they saw the organised parties, armed troops and police, who had taken longer to arrive, slowly advancing in a semi-circle round them. Any attempt at resistance would have ended in hurt to the women and children. Major Pritchard had no choice but to surrender.

Their feat created a sensation in Italy. The whole area was at once barred to neutrals, and there is no doubt that considerable consternation was caused. One Italian official announcement went so far as to say that it was impossible to conceal the fact that military circles considered the attempt a complete failure. Why it should have been thought necessary to conceal it was not explained.

First Visit to Lofoten

The parachute raid on Southern Italy was at that time an isolated experiment outside the general programme of raids. Shortly before it took place, the Commandos were divided—three (Nos. 7, 8 and 11) being sent to the Middle East where, together with two locally raised Commandos, they were formed into a force known as "Layforce" under Colonel (now Brigadier) R. E. Laycock, Royal Horse Guards. Their fortunes will be discussed later. Three weeks after the parachute attacks on the shores of the Mediterranean, the Commandos paid their first visit to the Lofoten Islands, close to the Arctic Circle.

The Lofoten Islands had with the rest of Norway fallen into German hands in the early summer of 1940. The herring- and cod-oil factories situated in the four ports of Stamsund, Henningsvaer, Svolvaer and Brettesnes had been taken over by the enemy and were supplying him with a product of which he stood in great need. It was decided to send a combined force to destroy the factories, capture the quislings and their German masters, and enlist recruits for the Norwegian Forces. Any ships found in the ports would be taken or sunk. The naval forces, under the command of Captain C. Caslon, R.N., consisted of five destroyers, the "Somali," the "Bedouin," the "Tartar," the "Eskimo" and the "Legion." They were escort to two infantry landing ships commanded by Commander J. Brunton, R.N., and Commander C. A. Kershaw, R.N., carrying No. 3 and No. 4 Commandos and some Royal Engineers. The military force commander was Brigadier (now Major-General) J. C. Haydon, D.S.O., O.B.E., commanding the Special Service

Brigade into which the Commandos had been formed. A detachment
of Norwegian soldiers and naval ratings, under their own officers, took
part in this raid, in the planning of which Norwegian officers collaborated.

The raiding force assembled, and waited a week while its commanders perfected their plans. These were not easy to make, for though,
as it chanced, there was to be no fighting ashore, this could not be
known beforehand, and arrangements had to be made to deal with
opposition during the landings, and with any enemy naval forces there

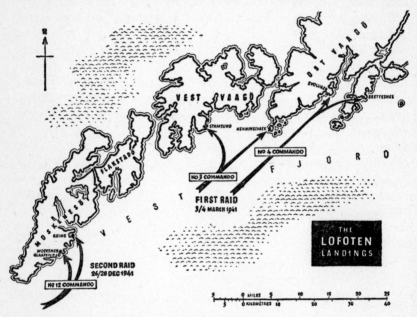

might be in the neighbourhood. The tortuous nature of the approaches
to the ports would make it impossible for the destroyers to come close
inshore to give covering fire if it were needed. The leading landing craft
were therefore ordered to act as scouts so that all would not be subjected
to fire at one and the same moment. The troops were also given sufficient
rations to enable them to remain ashore for 48 hours, if necessary, should
the escorting destroyers be forced to leave the neighbourhood of the
islands in order to fight a naval action.

The raiders, with a Norwegian pilot on board each ship, entered Vest
Fjord on the night of Monday, 3rd March, 1941, and at three o'clock
in the morning "the many navigational lights in the neighbourhood of

the Lofotens came into view." That they were burning seemed to show that the arrival of the force had been unheralded. This was so; the surprise was complete. The navigation of the Royal Navy had been as brilliant as the sunshine which gilded the landing craft when they moved away from their parent ships over the tumbling waters of the fjord towards the snow-covered islands ahead. Though the sun shone so brightly, it was very cold. "I was wearing two vests, two pullovers, a shirt, a Gieves' waistcoat, a wool-lined mackintosh and a pair of fur-lined boots," says one of those who took part, "and I was still cold."

Four landings were made, No. 3 Commando going ashore at Stamsund and Henningsvaer, and No. 4 at Svolvaer and Brettesnes. At no point was any opposition encountered, while the inhabitants welcomed our men very warmly. Gifts were exchanged, and it says much for the great spirit of the Norwegians that, far from resenting the demolitions which could not but destroy the livelihood of many of them, they were anxious and eager to help. Three hundred and fifteen volunteers, including eight women and the English manager of the firm of Allen and Hanbury, joined the expedition and returned to England with it. It had been originally intended to take back men only: but one of the English officers reported by wireless that there were eight Norwegian ladies anxious to join the Norwegian Red Cross. Could we take them off? Permission was granted. He related afterwards how one girl with her mother accompanied him to the landing stage, but her mother would not allow her to leave. She therefore turned back reluctantly for home, but before saying farewell gave him three presents, a handkerchief, a lock of her hair, and a kiss.

"I Got a Bleeding General"

The prisoners captured numbered two hundred and twenty-five, including ten quislings rounded up by the Norwegian detachment. One of these, possibly their chief, was the head of the local police. He was very splendidly dressed in a fine frock coat and an astrakhan hat. When taken, he became transported with fury and fear, which increased on coming alongside H.M.S. "Tartar." His guard—a short man compared with the tall quisling—caught sight of a friend on the destroyer's deck. "Hi, pal," he shouted, "look what I got here. Turn round, Albert." Then, pointing to the tall policeman, "Look, I got a bleeding General!"

The demolitions on shore were carried out by the party of Royal Engineers. They destroyed eleven cod- and herring-oil or fish-meal factories, an electric-light plant and all the oil tanks with their contents, 800,000 gallons. Five ships of a maximum tonnage of 18,900 were destroyed, four of them by a naval demolition party, and the fifth, the ss. "Hamburg"—a large factory and refrigerator ship of 9,780 tons—by the gunfire of H.M.S. "Tartar."

At sea the only opposition came from an armed trawler, the "Krebbs," sighted soon after 6 a.m. sailing out of Stamsund. Despite the odds, she showed fight and courageously engaged the headquarter ship, H.M.S. "Somali," which soon set her on fire. She ran aground on a small island, drifted off three hours later, and surrendered. Her survivors were taken prisoner and she was sunk by gunfire. Her captain had been killed at the beginning of the engagement. The prisoners were astonished at the treatment they received, for they had expected something very different. It had, they said, been front-page news in Germany that the captain of the "Cossack" had shot the whole crew of the "Altmark."

Very soon after the start of the operation the local Norwegian fishing fleet put to sea, and presently, in the words of the Naval Commander's report, "there were literally hundreds of little fishing smacks and small puffers beginning to fish in the adjacent waters. It quickly became clear to them that our operations were directed against the Germans and that they were not to be molested. They showed their friendliness and enthusiasm by cheering and waving and hoisting Norwegian flags." They also loaded the decks of the "Somali" with freshly-caught fish while she lay stopped during the boarding and searching of the trawler "Krebbs."

By 1 p.m. the troops had re-embarked and the expedition sailed for home, leaving behind it the wreckage of the herring- and cod-oil industry in that part of Norway and a number of valuable merchant ships at the bottom of the fjord. It reached Scapa unmolested, exactly two days later.

Spitzbergen Goes Off the Air

The opening of the German campaign against the U.S.S.R. on the 22nd June, 1941, caused the far northern seas of Europe to assume an importance which they had not possessed since the evacuation of Narvik, a year previously.

Three hundred and seventy miles from the most northern point of Norway, to which it belongs, lies the Spitzbergen archipelago. The coal deposits of Spitzbergen had been exploited for more than 40 years by various Norwegian and international companies, the Norwegian mines in Long Year City having handled, for the last 20 years, the greatest output. The main island, West Spitzbergen, also has very rich coal deposits which were opened up in 1931 by a Soviet coal company, employing about 2,000 Soviet citizens out of a total population of some 2,800. An agreement was reached by Great Britain, the U.S.S.R. and Norway in July 1941, that immediate steps should be taken to deny the Spitzbergen coal to Germany. It was not thought desirable to maintain a permanent garrison in the islands. What could be done was so to disable the mines as to ensure that the Germans could derive no benefit from them, to destroy any stocks of coal and evacuate the inhabitants.

On the 25th August, 1941, there arrived in Spitzbergen a small force of Canadian troops under the command of Brigadier A. E. Potts, escorted by units of the Royal Navy under Rear-Admiral P. L. Vian, D.S.O. It consisted of a company of Royal Canadian Engineers, detachments of the Edmonton Regiment, the Saskatoon Light Infantry and the Royal Canadian Corps of Signals, and some details. With them were some small detachments of United Kingdom troops, including a party of the Royal Engineers and a detachment of Norwegian soldiers, under a staff officer who took local command in Long Year City and arranged for the transfer of the Norwegian population. Many of the Canadians had formed part of an expedition which was organised to attack Trondhjem in April 1940 but never sailed. The military forces had spent some time at a Combined Operations Training Centre in Scotland, becoming familiar with various landing craft and learning the technique of making a landing on beaches held by the enemy.

No opposition from the enemy was encountered, however, and the force anchored in Green Harbour in the Ice Sound of West Spitzbergen. The inhabitants showed great friendliness, and immediate preparations were made to evacuate them, the Soviet citizens to the U.S.S.R., the Norwegians to England. Once the former had been got aboard, the demolition parties went to work. Essential parts of the mining machinery were removed or destroyed. A disused wireless station was blown up and the overhead conveyor system, bringing the coal from one of the largest mines to the dock side, was destroyed. 450,000 tons of coal lying in ordered heaps were set on fire together with 275,000 gallons of fuel oil, petrol and grease. "Exploding barrels," states an eye-witness, "were seen rising to a height of about 250 feet and were thrown out from the pile, flaming, to a distance of from 350 to 400 feet."

The Norwegian population were then evacuated, and as the last of them reached the ships, the transport which had gone to a northern Russian port with the Soviet miners returned with some 200 French officers and men on board. They had escaped to the U.S.S.R. from German prison camps and were eager to fight under General de Gaulle. Their reception by the British and Canadian military and naval officers brought tears to their eyes. "Every moment," writes one of them, "brought us new proofs of an affection for us far beyond the brotherhood of arms. Those of us who knew nothing of English tact learnt that it is shown by the smallest of gestures as well as by the most generous gifts. We had hardly arrived when English and Canadian officers knocked on our cabin doors and brought one of their own uniforms to each French officer, so that he might make himself, at last, presentable."

The final task was the destruction of the two wireless stations. Throughout the period of our occupation, they had been transmitting their normal weather reports, so that the enemy might suspect nothing. This deception was completely successful, for no German air reconnaissance came anywhere near the islands. They may well have hesitated to do so, because on several occasions the wireless stations reported fog conditions which did not, in fact, exist. The Germans knew nothing about the expedition until it was over: when it was on its way back, on the night of the 3rd/4th September, their station at Tromsö could be heard urgently calling Spitzbergen and demanding, in vain, an answer.

5. THE EXPLOITS OF "LAYFORCE"

As has already been recorded, the Special Service troops were split up in the autumn of 1940, three Commandos being sent to Egypt where it was hoped that they would arrive in time to take part in General Wavell's offensive against Graziani. They went in three infantry landing ships and arrived in March, 1941. The end of the month saw them a compact force under Colonel (now Brigadier) R. E. Laycock, rehearsing for an operation which had subsequently to be cancelled when the arrival in Libya of strong German reinforcements under Rommel robbed us of the initiative. It was decided, however, that something less ambitious could be undertaken with profit, and the enemy's base at Bardia was chosen as the objective. It was raided on the night of 19th/20th April by No. 7 Commando and a small detachment of the Royal Tank Regiment. Serving as a volunteer with the Commando was Admiral Sir W. H. Cowan, Bt., K.C.B., D.S.O., M.V.O., who, at the age of seventy-one, did not consider his period of active service at an end. On this raid he fell into a deep ditch, and being a man of small stature, found some difficulty in getting out; his efforts to do so were, in his view, severely handicapped by those of friends nearby who sought to help him. When Layforce was disbanded he joined some Indian Cavalry, and was captured after a hand-to-hand fight on 27th May, 1941.

The raid on Bardia was a considerable strategic success. Alarmed by it, the enemy diverted the greater part of a German armoured brigade from Sollum, where it was beginning to exert heavy pressure, and kept it for some time in the neighbourhood of Bardia.

The expedition to this town appeared to show that considerable advantage could be gained by following a programme of small-scale raids on the enemy's lines of communication, which ran for so many miles along or near the coast. He would thus be kept in a state of apprehension about his communications—and communications are of vital importance to any army, especially one which is operating in the inhospitable desert at great distance from its bases.

Three factors, however, prevented the use of the Commandos for this purpose. A fortnight before the raid on Bardia, the Axis powers

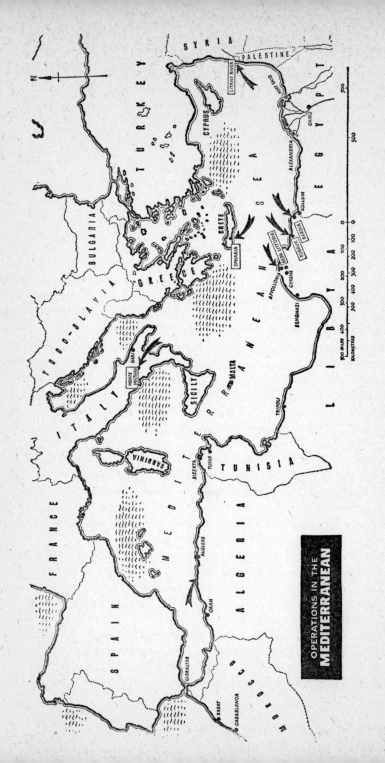

OPERATIONS IN THE
MEDITERRANEAN

had begun their advance through Yugoslavia and Greece, and the whole situation in the Eastern Mediterranean soon underwent a change for the worse. The best troops of our Army in North Africa had to be sent to the help of the hard-pressed Greeks. Their task against the weight of a far more numerous and more heavily-armed German Army—the Italians did not count—was from the very beginning impossible, and after heavy fighting they had to be withdrawn. Shipping to take them off was the main problem, and everything which would float had to be pressed into service. The infantry landing ships were therefore diverted from their original role, sent to Greece, and suffered considerable damage from the fire of the enemy. They were not, therefore, available for transporting the Commandos to the scene of action.

Moreover, the enemy's air activity in the area off the north coast of Africa was daily increasing, and soon made operations by any craft slower than a destroyer exceedingly hazardous, unless fighter protection could be provided—an impossibility at that moment. Lastly, our armies in the Middle East were becoming seriously short of men to such an extent that the Commandos were soon the only troops in general reserve. Thus, through a combination of circumstances which must always arise in warfare when one of the two sides has to engage in operations beyond its strength, trained assault troops had to be used for a purpose for which they were not originally intended.

Rearguard Action at Sphakia

No. 11 Commando was sent to Cyprus to form part of its garrison. Nos. 7 and 8, with the two locally raised Commandos, were kept as general reserve. They were soon in action. The fight was going against us in Crete, and in the third week of May it became necessary to withdraw what remained of its garrison. The four Commandos were put into the island with orders to fight a rearguard action. The first attempt to get there failed. They went in four destroyers, in weather which grew steadily worse. The whole of Crete was found to be covered by a thick pall of low cloud, and in the pitch darkness no landfall was made. On their way they had passed the wounded "Kipling" with survivors of the "Kashmir" and the "Kelly" on board. These two destroyers had been sunk after much fighting close inshore off Crete. The "Kelly" had been commanded by the future chief of Combined Operations, who was one of the survivors. These four Commandos returned to Alexandria, immediately transhipped to four more destroyers and went back. This time, led by Colonel Laycock, they landed successfully at Sphakia on the night of the 26th/27th May.

They were very unsuitably equipped to fight a rearguard action, for they had no artillery or mortars. There were tommy guns and rifles in plenty, and some sixteen Bren guns, but these are not the best weapons to use in a retreat, where the action should be fought by the retreating troops, as far as possible, with weapons capable of causing the enemy to deploy before he can come up with them. Dawn found the force holding a defensive position astride the main road inland from Sphakia. They expected to be heavily dive-bombed, and their expectations were fulfilled. The men stood up to this experience very well, and in point of fact the casualties caused were exceedingly light. The Commandos found that the physical effect of dive-bombing bears no relation to the effect which it may have on the nerves. As one of them remarked at the time: "Do you remember what the old lady said in the middle of a blitz? There is something to be said for these bombs—they do take your mind off the war." The general opinion of this dive-bombing was expressed by Captain Evelyn Waugh, who, after experiencing it for some time, said that like all things German it was very efficient and went on much too long.

From the morning of the 27th until the night of the 31st May, the Commandos fought a rearguard action which enabled the main evacuation at Sphakia to take place. They were constantly surrounded by day, but were able to get away at night, for they found that the Germans did not move much after darkness. The right technique was soon discovered. Before dusk one or two light counter-attacks by seven or eight men were made, and these sufficed to keep the enemy quiet throughout the night which followed.

On the 28th, Colonel Laycock, with his headquarters, was ambushed. By then he had three tanks with him. "By the most fortunate chance," he says, "the ambush was close to the three tanks and the Germans did not see them. The enemy were about 30 yards or less away from us when my Brigade-Major and I jumped into a tank and drove straight over the Germans." They rejoined the main body, presenting a strange appearance, for the tanks were still swathed in the camouflage netting with which they had been covered.

The fighting that day was heavy, but the Germans were beaten off and did not again attack in force. The difficulties, however, on the beach at Sphakia were such that, by the time it was the turn of the

Commandos to be taken off, very few craft were available. Our vessels had suffered heavy losses in performing what must always be a sad task for assault craft—that of carrying out the inverted type of combined operation known as evacuation. Many officers and men had to be left behind and, in all, their casualties in killed, wounded and missing amounted to some 600, or three-quarters of their strength. A few got back in a landing craft which, when the petrol gave out, they took to North Africa by means of a sail made of blankets lashed together with boot laces. The passage took six days.

The four Commandos had fought with great tenacity and had served their purpose, having enabled some thousands of the exhausted garrison of Crete to be carried off by the Royal Navy into Egypt, where they were subsequently to give so good an account of themselves in the ranks of the Eighth Army.

The Twin Pimples of Tobruk

A detachment of No. 8 Commando, consisting of five officers and 70 other ranks, was shortly afterwards sent to Tobruk to carry out small raids as opportunity offered. Its fortunes are best illustrated by recounting one very successful raid made on the 18th July.

The objective was a position known as the Twin Pimples—a strong point consisting of two small hills close together. These were held by part of the Italian Force besieging Tobruk, which from there dominated the forward positions of the 18th Indian Cavalry on the perimeter opposite. It was decided that the Italian garrison of this post, a thorn in the flesh of the Indians, must be wiped out. For some days before the raid, officers and men of No. 8.Commando went out with the Indians on patrol in the desert in order to become thoroughly familiar with the ground. They learnt much from their Indian comrades, whose skill in moving at night over ground held or dominated by an enemy is proverbial.

The plan for the attack on the Twin Pimples was to slip through the Italian forward positions, then through their main positions as far as the main road or track up which supplies to the garrison were taken. The Commando would then turn to the right, move along the track, and take the Italians in the rear. Three minutes before the assault on the Twin Pimples was delivered, the 18th Indian Cavalry were to carry out a diversion against the forward Italian posts.

The night of the 18th July was dark, but it must be remembered that

darkness in the desert is never as great as it is in England. The assaulting party consisted of Captain M. Keely, Devonshire Regiment, in
command, with Captain P. Dunne, Royal Horse Guards, as second-in-
command, Lieutenant J. S. Lewis, Welsh Guards, and 40 other ranks.
Half were armed with tommy guns and half with rifles and bayonets.
All had hand grenades, and every third man carried a ground sheet worn
bandolier fashion, to be used as a stretcher if necessary.

Zero hour was 1 a.m. and the attackers, starting two hours earlier
in battle formation, took with them a number of Australian Sappers to
blow up any ammunition dumps or mortars which might be discovered.
"We walked briskly," says Captain Dunne in his account: "It was like
an English summer evening and very pleasant. We moved in complete
silence, being particularly careful not to betray ourselves by coughing.
We were all wearing rubber boots. We went through the Italian forward
positions and then through their main defensive lines. I shall never
know if they were manned or not because we heard nothing from them
and were very careful to make no noise."

Having reached the track they waited a short time, and then turned
right-handed and moved to the rear of the Twin Pimples. As they drew
near it, the diversion staged by the 18th Indian Cavalry Regiment began.
The Italians opened fire against the Indians and sent up Very lights.
Their attention was fully occupied, and the Commandos got within 30
yards before they were challenged. They formed up in line immediately
and went forward firing their tommy guns and rifles. "The fight lasted
about three or four minutes. In order that we should not fight each other
in the dark, we used a password 'Jock,' and I heard 'Jock,' 'Jock' being
shouted all over the place, mingling with the sound of rifle shots and
the explosion of grenades. The Italians rushed into their dugouts and we
bombed them out." The Australian Sappers blew up the ammunition
dumps and several trench mortars.

The attackers then withdrew, finding their direction by the brilliant
stars. They had reckoned that not more than a quarter of an hour
would elapse before the Italian artillery would realise what was happening and shell the Twin Pimples. This calculation was exact. They left
at the end of fifteen minutes and "were only about a hundred yards
away from the position when the enemy began to plaster it with everything they had." Our only casualties were one man mortally wounded
and four wounded. One of these got back unaided, though his arm was
broken and he had a bullet in his leg. The success of this attack was

largely due to the careful methods of reconnaissance learnt from the Indians.

Commandos in Syria: the Litani River Crossing

No. 11 Commando, it will be remembered, had been sent to Cyprus to form part of its garrison. They, too, were shortly to be in action, taking part in the melancholy campaign of Syria. This French mandated territory, which at the fall of France had passed under the control of the pro-Nazi Government of Vichy, was eventually occupied by the Allies on 11th July, 1941, but not without heavy fighting, much of which was borne by the Australians. After a fairly swift initial advance, they found themselves held up by the Litani River at a point which was strongly defended by some detachments of the French Colonial Army, among them the 22nd Tirailleurs from Algeria. The Australians had reached the point at which the river flows into the sea. Near its mouth was a bridge at a place called Kafr Bada. It was here that the Vichy troops were established in a strong redoubt. It was decided to put No. 11 Commando ashore to capture the redoubt, seize the bridge and thus enable the Australians to advance once more.

The first attempt was made on the night of the 7th/8th June. The infantry landing ship arrived off the mouth of the river, having on board 27 officers and 456 other ranks of No. 11 Commando. They were under the command of Lieutenant-Colonel R. R. H. Pedder, Major (subsequently Lieutenant-Colonel) G. C. T. Keyes being second-in-command. There was a full moon, so that the night was almost as light as day, and there is little doubt that the infantry landing ship, with her escort of destroyers, H.M.S. "Ilex" and H.M.S. "Hotspur," was seen. There was a very considerable surf running on the beach, and though the landing craft were successfully lowered, they did not take the troops ashore. They were about to do so when Lieutenant F. H. Colenut, R.N.V.R., who had once been a policeman in Palestine, and possessed a considerable local knowledge of the coast, hailed the Captain of the infantry landing ship from a patrol launch, and said that any attempt to land would be disastrous. The force therefore returned to Port Said. No sooner had it arrived than it was ordered to sea again with instructions to carry out the operation that same night.

Lieutenant-Colonel Pedder had decided to land his men in three detachments on the north side of the mouth of the Litani River, and strike inland with the object of taking the French defences in their right flank. He took this decision as a result of an intelligence report which stated that the French had blown up the bridge at Kafr Bada, and withdrawn their detachments from the south side of the river. The landing took place at dawn, the Commandos going in in their craft with the setting moon behind them and a rising sun in front. Lieutenant-Colonel Pedder who was with the centre detachment, and Captain G. R. M. H. More commanding the left, were successfully landed on the north side of the river. Major Keyes with his men found themselves put ashore by mistake on the south side. Lieutenant-Colonel Pedder with his men at once advanced and was soon heavily engaged. He was shot through the head, the other officers wounded, and the Company Sergeant-Major assumed command. Under him the detachment went forward, captured the local barracks, and thus prevented reinforcements from moving up to strengthen the redoubt which was the key-point of the defence.

Captain More's detachment, which had met with very little opposition to begin with, captured a number of howitzers and French 75 field guns. The fighting became heavy and confused and at one time the prisoners taken by the Commando greatly outnumbered their captors. As the day wore on, the Commando found itself in a very exposed position and under heavy fire. The initial advantage, gained by the confusion into which the enemy had been thrown by their attack, had largely been lost. It was at this moment that Major Keyes, son of Admiral of the Fleet Sir Roger Keyes, at that time Director of Combined Operations, arrived to take command.

He and his men had had to cross the river, having been landed on the wrong side. This he realised after catching sight of the masts of a number of feluccas, which he perceived were to the north of him when they should have been to the south. Under a heavy barrage from French 75's, mortars and machine guns, his detachment reached the river bank. Here, under the same fire, which caused a number of casualties, they succeeded in crossing the river in driblets in a boat borrowed from the Australians and paddled to and fro between bank and bank. Once on the other side, Major Keyes organised the attack on the redoubt and about one o'clock captured it.

No. 11 Commando lost in this action 123 officers and other ranks, killed and missing, or some twenty-five per cent. of its strength. There is no doubt that its capture of this strongly-held position proved of very great importance at a critical moment in the campaign.

6. A STROKE AT THE BRAIN: THE RAID ON ROMMEL

After this engagement No. 11 Commando returned to Cyprus, while the other Commandos, with the exception of the detachment from No. 8 at Tobruk, were concentrated near Alexandria. By now they had suffered many casualties and the problem of replacement had become acute. No men were available from units in the Middle East, which were already well below their war establishments. The decision was therefore taken, with great reluctance, to disband Layforce. Some of them returned to their original units, others to the United Kingdom, and others remained to become the nucleus of a small reconstituted force formed to wage amphibious warfare in the Mediterranean. It was part of that force which carried out the action now to be described.

Early in October six officers and 53 other ranks of the Scottish Commando were placed under the operational command of the Eighth Army. It was decided to use them in a bold and daring attempt to strike at the brain of the enemy by landing far behind his lines and attacking his headquarters. Four detachments were formed for this purpose: the first to raid General Rommel's house at Beda Littoria; the second to assault the Italian headquarters at Cyrene; the third, the Italian Intelligence centre at Appollonia; while a fourth detachment was to cut telephone and telegraph communications.

The first problem was how to get the Force to its destination. It was not possible to use destroyers, for the risk of air attack was too great, and it was therefore decided to take them in two submarines, H.M.S. "Torbay" and H.M.S. "Talisman." On reaching their immediate destination they would paddle themselves ashore in rubber boats.

On the evening of the 10th November, the "Torbay" and the "Talisman" slipped and sailed from Alexandria, moving westward in fair weather, without incident. The Scottish Commando was in the highest spirits. "All ranks were greatly interested," runs the official report, "in what was to us a novel method of approaching our objective, and the soldiers were high in their praise of the way in which they were fed and accommodated." The first landing was made from H.M.S. "Torbay," which closed the chosen beach at dusk on the 14th November. That the submarine reached her exact destination without undue difficulty was due not only to sound navigation, but also to the calculated daring of a British officer, Captain (now Lieutenant-Colonel) J. E. Haselden, who, dressed as an Arab, had been moving behind the enemy's lines and had established friendly relations with some of the local inhabitants. His signals from the beach were seen, and preparations to land the Scottish Commando began. The weather was deteriorating; the wind had freshened, and the swell was now considerable. Four of the rubber boats were washed away, and much time was lost retrieving them. Eventually the landing was successfully made; but, instead of the estimated one hour, it took five to accomplish.

Meanwhile H.M.S. "Talisman" was lying some distance off, awaiting the signal that the landings from H.M.S. "Torbay" had been completed. The weather got worse and worse, and Colonel Laycock had just decided to postpone the operation until the following night, when the expected signal from the "Torbay" was received. The landing from the "Talisman" took place in a heavy sea which capsized most of the boats, throwing the men into the water. All of them, with the exception of Colonel Laycock and seven other ranks who reached the shore, swam back to the submarine.

Once ashore, Colonel Laycock and his small party, which had now joined those who had landed from H.M.S. "Torbay," took cover in a convenient wadi for the remainder of the night and for the day which followed. The weather continued bad with a considerable sea still running, and it did not seem possible that the "Talisman" would be able to land troops when darkness came. On the other hand, General Auchinleck's offensive against Rommel was about to open, and Colonel Laycock was well aware that any immediate action he could take against the enemy would be of great and immediate value to the Eighth Army now making ready to advance.

One Minute to Midnight

He decided not to wait, but had therefore to modify his plan and divide the party into two detachments. Lieutenant-Colonel Keyes, in command of the first detachment, was to attack the German headquarters and the house of General Rommel. He had with him Captain Campbell and 17 other ranks. The second detachment, Lieutenant Cook and six other ranks, was ordered to cut the telephone and telegraph wires at the cross-roads south of Cyrene. Colonel Laycock decided to remain at the rendezvous with a sergeant and two men, to form a beach-head and keep the reserve ammunition and rations. They would also be ready to receive the remainder of the Commando, who, it was hoped, would be put ashore on the following night.

Thus did Colonel Laycock and his officers plan through that long day hidden in the wadi. The weather was at no time good, and became very bad as the hours went by. A gale of wind, accompanied at times by torrential rain, howled through their place of concealment, and soon everyone was once more wet to the skin.

The detachments moved off at seven o'clock in the evening, accompanied by Arab guides who, however, abandoned them after a few miles. They therefore lay up in a suitable wadi and slept for four hours. The next day they hid in another, and in the evening, meeting with a party of Arabs who were friendly, were guided to a spot some ten miles from Beda Littoria, where they dumped their surplus clothing and rations. On both those nights Colonel Laycock visited the beach, but there was still a heavy surf and conditions for landing were impossible.

At seven in the evening of the 17th November, the detachments made ready to move to their objectives. Torrential rain had fallen all day; they were cold and soaked to the skin, but their spirit was high. No. 1 detachment under Lieutenant-Colonel Keyes was guided to within a few hundred yards of General Rommel's headquarters by friendly Arabs. Here they lay up awaiting zero hour, which was one minute to midnight, and while there they were apprehended by a party of Arabs in uniform. Captain Campbell, however, allayed suspicion by explaining in German that the force belonged to a German unit.

The plan was for Lieutenant-Colonel Keyes, with Captain Campbell and Sergeant Terry, to enter the house of the German Commander-in-Chief and search it. Outside, three men were to destroy the electric-light plant, five to keep an eye on the garden and the car park, two to stand outside a nearby hotel and prevent anyone from leaving it, and two more to watch the road on each side of the house. The two remaining men were to guard whichever way Lieutenant-Colonel Keyes chose for entering the house.

Everyone was in position a little before midnight. The house was reconnoitred, but no way in could be found either through the back or through any of the windows. Lieutenant-Colonel Keyes and his com-

panions therefore went up to the front door and beat upon it, Captain
Campbell loudly demanding in German that it should be opened. Inside
was a sentry. Hearing a peremptory order shouted at him from outside,
he pulled open the door and was at once set upon. He showed fight and
was overpowered, but not silently; Captain Campbell was compelled to
shoot him, and the shot roused the house. Two men began to run downstairs from the first floor, but a burst of tommy-gun fire from Sergeant
Terry sent them scampering back again. The lights in the rooms of the
ground floor were extinguished, but no one attempted to move.

Lieutenant-Colonel Keyes and Captain Campbell began a search of
the ground floor. There was no one in the first room, but in the second
the Germans were awaiting them, and on throwing open the door
Lieutenant-Colonel Keyes was met by a burst of fire and fell back into
the passage, mortally wounded. Sergeant Terry emptied three magazines of his tommy gun into the darkened room; Captain Campbell
threw a grenade into it and then slammed the door. He and Sergeant
Terry picked up Lieutenant-Colonel Keyes and carried him outside,
where he died. He received the posthumous award of the Victoria Cross.
While bending over him, Captain Campbell had his leg broken by a
stray bullet.

Rommel Was Not at Home

The enemy had been taken by surprise, but most unfortunately General Rommel himself was absent. He was apparently attending a party
in Rome. Three German Lieutenant-Colonels on his staff were killed
and a number of soldiers killed and wounded. Captain Campbell ordered Sergeant Terry to collect the detachment and throw all their remaining grenades through the windows. This was done, and Captain
Campbell then ordered the party to withdraw and to leave him behind,
since in his wounded condition they could not hope to carry him over 18
miles of difficult country to the beach. He was taken prisoner. The
party moved off, being joined by the three men detailed to destroy the
electric-lighting plant. In this they had been partially successful, though
some of the charges, soaked by the torrential rain, had not exploded. A
grenade placed in the armature had, however, done considerable damage. Sergeant Terry led his party back and eventually reached Colonel
Laycock at the rendezvous on the evening of the 18th November.

Meanwhile the other detachment had reached the cross-roads of

Cyrene and blown up a petrol-distribution post. They never returned to the rendezvous.

In the hour of daylight still remaining after the arrival of Sergeant Terry, Colonel Laycock went to the beach and saw with relief that the swell was diminishing. The rubber boats, however, in which the party had come ashore and which had been hidden in a cave, had been moved by friendly Arabs, who had then departed without indicating the whereabouts of the new hiding place.

Shortly after dark, Colonel Laycock sighted H.M.S. "Torbay" and flashed her a message. A long wait ensued, and then the friendly Arabs turned up. They had stowed the boats in some caves, which Colonel Laycock was examining when the look-out ran up to say that the "Torbay" was now signalling. Back went Colonel Laycock to the beach—he was the only one of the party who could read Morse—and learnt from the winking lamp of the submarine that the sea was too rough, and that she would try again the following night. The Colonel in his reply told them of the attempt on Rommel's headquarters and of the death of Lieutenant-Colonel Keyes. The "Torbay" then moved off after successfully floating ashore a rubber boat with food and water. This was thankfully received, and the party prepared to spend the remainder of the night and the next day on shore, praying for better weather.

At first light, a defensive position was adopted, the main detachment remaining near the caves, while two smaller detachments protected the eastern and western flanks of the position. The morning wore on; all was quiet; the wind and sea were abating; the hopes of the party were rising. But, at noon, shots were heard. They came from the westernmost sentry group, who were in action against some Italian native levies, known to be in the neighbourhood. Colonel Laycock was not unduly worried. He felt confident that he and his men would be able to keep off the Arabs until darkness, and then retire to the beach. Two small parties were sent out to outflank the enemy, but did not succeed in doing so, for by now German troops had appeared, while beyond them was a considerable party of Italians. These remained on the sky-line about a mile to the north, and took no part in the fighting.

One of the small parties returned, having been able to advance about a quarter of a mile and come into action. After their tommy gun jammed, the officer with them, Lieutenant Prior, continued to advance alone until wounded. With great difficulty he crawled back to the main position.

The Germans were by now maintaining a sustained fire, and it became evident about two o'clock in the afternoon that it would be impossible to hold the beach against such superior forces. The only alternative was to abandon the position, hide in the Jebel, the broken hills in the interior, and await the advance of the Eighth Army. When the enemy were no more than 200 yards from the caves, Colonel Laycock ordered the detachment to split up into small parties, dash across the open and seek the cover of the hills inland. There they could either try to get in touch with H.M.S. "Talisman," which they knew would be lying off an alternative beach that night, or they could hide in the wadis which abounded, and await our forces. Lieutenant Prior, who was grievously wounded, was left behind with a medical orderly and ordered to surrender. The party then scattered.

Colonel Laycock found himself with Sergeant Terry. They crossed half a mile of open country, being continually sniped, but neither of them was hit. Once in the shelter of the Jebel, which offered excellent cover, they set out together to join the Eighth Army. After the first few days they made friends with various members of the local Senoussi tribes, who helped them and hid them each night in the very wadis which the enemy were known to have searched during the day. "Our greatest problem," wrote Colonel Laycock, "was the lack of food, and though never desperate we were forced to subsist for periods, which never exceeded two-and-a-half consecutive days, on berries only, and we became appreciably weak from want of nourishment. At other times we fed well on goat and Arab bread, but developed a marked craving for sugar. Water never presented a serious proposition as it rained practically continuously."

One evening they were making a thin stew out of some meat and bones—mostly bones—which they had flavoured with wild garlic picked by Colonel Laycock. As they were about to eat it a friendly Arab arrived, gave one loud sniff, and overturned the pot. He subsequently explained to the enraged and hungry pair that the garlic would have destroyed their sight.

Eventually the colonel and the sergeant joined the British Forces at Cyrene, 41 days after they had originally set out. They were the only members of the party to do so. It was Christmas Day, 1941, and having eaten his Christmas dinner, Colonel Laycock flew to Cairo to make his report.

7. THE SIGNIFICANT ADVENTURE OF VAAGSO

On the 27th October, 1941, Admiral of the Fleet Sir Roger Keyes was succeeded as Director of Combined Operations by Captain the Lord Louis Mountbatten, G.C.V.O., D.S.O., A.D.C., who was promoted Commodore First Class, and on the 18th March, 1942, Acting Vice-Admiral, when his title was changed to Chief of Combined Operations. At the same time he was granted honorary commissions in the Army as a Lieutenant-General and in the Royal Air Force as an Air Marshal. He at once set about planning a raid on a part of the occupied coast of Europe where, it was hoped, the enemy would least expect to be attacked. The country chosen was Norway, the place Vaagso, some hundreds of miles south of the Lofoten Islands so successfully visited in the previous March.

The object of the raid was, while harassing the German defences on the coast of South-West Norway, to attack and destroy a number of military and economic targets in the town of South Vaagso and on the nearby island of Maaloy, and to capture or sink any shipping found in Ulvesund. Ulvesund is the name borne by the strip of water on which the port of Vaagso lies and which divides the island of that name from the mainland. It forms part of the Indreled, that narrow passage which stretches along so much of the coast of Norway, and is in the nature of a more or less continuous channel bounded by a chain of islands on the one hand and the mainland of Norway on the other. Through the Indreled passes most of the coastwise traffic, for, by so doing, ships can use the protection afforded by the chain of islands. At certain points the Indreled is broken, and one of these is situated at the north end of Ulvesund at a point where it joins a wide bay. Ships sailing northward must cross this bay and double the peninsula of Stadtlandet, to the south of which lies the island of Vaagso. They tend, therefore, to congregate in Ulvesund, where they remain awaiting a suitable moment to pass into the open sea round the end of Stadtlandet, which is noted for its storms, and then northwards once more under the cover of the

49

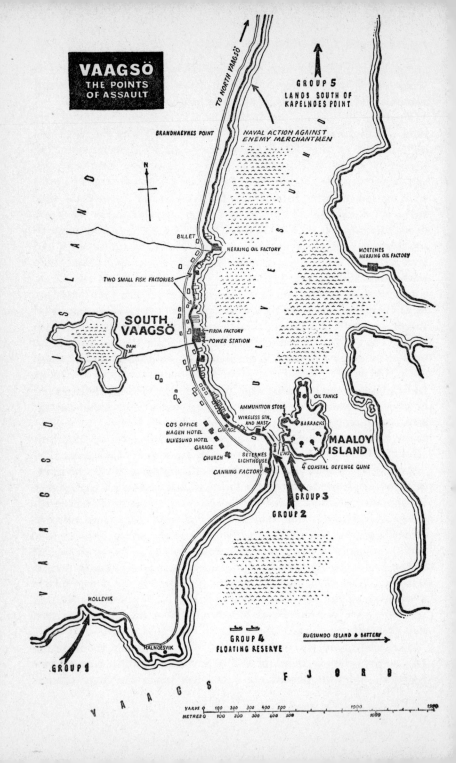

numerous islands. Running roughly at right angles to Ulvesund is Vaags Fjord; where the two stretches of water meet, there is a small island named Maaloy, opposite which is the town of South Vaagso.

The Germans had not forgotten to fortify the southern end of Ulvesund, and they had established coastal defences on the island of Maaloy itself, as well as in and near the town of South Vaagso opposite. On Maaloy, a battery of field guns had been mounted, and there were also anti-aircraft batteries and machine guns, while four miles to the southward was a battery of fairly heavy guns, possibly of French origin, situated on the island of Rugsundo; they were laid so as to fire westward down Vaags Fjord. Both Maaloy Island and South Vaagso were garrisoned by German troops, and it so happened that those in the town had been reinforced a few days before the attack by a detachment sent there to spend Christmas.

It was decided to approach the town and island up Vaags Fjord, the entrance of which is marked by two lighthouses at Hovdenoes and Bergsholmene. On reaching the small bay behind Halnoevik Point, south of the little village of Hollevik, a short distance from South Vaagso, the landing craft from the assault ships were to be lowered and landings made first under cover of a naval bombardment and then of smoke laid by aircraft. Once ashore, the island of Maaloy and the town of South Vaagso were to be captured and anything of value to the enemy, such as fish-oil factories, destroyed.

Strange Behaviour of a Table

After carrying out a number of rehearsals the force sailed on Christmas Eve, arriving at an anchorage on Christmas Day. Very heavy weather was met with. During the passage the secretary to the captain of one of the infantry landing ships invited his commanding officer to the cabin and showed him a table moving rhythmically up and down the wall, a distance of some six inches. It was eventually discovered that this levitation was due to the heavy seas, which were literally squeezing the sides of the ship. The infantry landing ships suffered some damage. This was repaired; but since the weather did not immediately abate, it was decided to postpone the operation for 24 hours. The men were, therefore, able to eat their Christmas dinner in comfort.

The weather having improved, the force sailed at four p.m. on Boxing Day with the promise of still further improvement. Nor was the promise belied; the storm died down, and by the time the Norwegian coast was reached, weather conditions were perfect. The ships moving across the North Sea out of the sunset into the darkness of the long winter night were a fine sight. On either side of the main formation destroyers kept guard, altering speed and course constantly. In the van was H.M.S. "Kenya," a six-inch cruiser, flying the flag of Rear-Admiral H. M. Burroughs, C.B., and in line astern behind him came the infantry landing ships. While it was still dark, landfall was made exactly at the estimated position and time. "We approached from the west into the promise of dawn," says one who was on the bridge of the "Kenya." "It was a very eerie sensation entering the fjord in absolute silence and very slowly. I wondered what was going to happen for it seemed that the ship had lost her proper element, that she was no longer a free ship at sea. Occasionally I saw a little hut with a light burning in it and I wondered whether that light would be suddenly switched off, which would mean that the enemy had spotted us, or whether it would continue to burn as some Norwegian fisherman got out of bed, stretched himself and went off to his nets."

Another standing beside him had much the same experience. "We lay down to sleep at the end of a rough evening with the ship moving uncomfortably and the wind noisy. When we woke up it was very still, and we went on deck with the usual holiday expectations of finding that overnight the scene had changed, that we had come to a new land to enjoy a promised excitement. The wind had gone; the sea was quiet—everything was completely quiet—there was a fine moon in a clear sky and, ahead, the first suggestion of morning twilight. The other ships were neatly in line astern, and the whole force appeared to be shut in by high, steep, snow-covered mountains. A long way above us, a window shone out brilliantly, the lovely sight of a lit window hung in the darkness; this was peace again.

"It was most disturbing that there was so little left to do because everything had been done beforehand. We noted the time, exactly one minute late, that the landing craft were lowered and could just be seen through glasses, black beetles crawling in the shadow of the mountains up the black waters of the fjord. We heard our aircraft overhead and saw their welcome of heavy, familiar tracer fire rising quite slowly from the surrounding slopes. Our ship was moving very quietly towards the headland where we should come into sight of the battery, which ought by now to be expecting our arrival. As we nosed round the point, everyone was waiting for the order to 'open the line of fire,' and get in first with a salvo. It should have been a thrilling moment; but all the same, it was difficult to look at anything except that nostalgic window, now high astern of us, still lit and still shining brightly in the dark morning."

Fifty Shells a Minute

The naval bombardment opened at 8.48 a.m., the "Kenya" firing a salvo of star shell which lit up the island of Maaloy, showing not only the target to the naval gunners, but also the place where they were to drop their smoke bombs to the crews of the Hampdens. This salvo was followed by further salvos of six-inch shells. Two minutes later the destroyers joined in the bombardment which lasted nine and a quarter minutes. During that brief period between four and five hundred six-inch shells fell upon a space not more than 250 yards square.

The Germans on the island had been caught unprepared. They were following their usual routine: the gunners were being roused by a loud-voiced N.C.O., the officer commanding was shaving, his batman, whose turn it was that morning to man the telephone connecting headquarters with the look-out post, was cleaning his officer's boots on the table beside the instrument. So busily engaged was he upon this task that he allowed the telephone bell to ring, and did not trouble to pick up the receiver. The German gunners thus received no warning. Outside the barracks on the island of Maaloy, there was a naval signalling station established on its highest point. The signaller on duty received a message flashed by lamp telling of the advent of our forces. He ran down to the small bay on the north side of the island, leapt into a boat and rowed as fast as he could to the headquarters of the German Naval Commandant on the main island of Vaagso. Here he delivered the warning, but when asked whether he had warned the army gunners on Maaloy he replied, "Oh, no, Sir; it is a military battery, and this is a naval signal." The Germans are a methodical people.

The landing craft carried troops belonging to No. 2 and No. 3 Commandos, a detachment of Royal Engineers from No. 6 Commando, and some men of the Royal Army Medical Corps from No. 4 Commando. With these British troops was a detachment of the Royal Norwegian Army. To this body of men, made up of 51 officers and 525 other ranks, five general tasks had been entrusted. For their fulfilment they were divided into five groups. Group 1 was to land near the village of Holle-vik, on the southern shore of the island of Vaagso and a short distance from the town of South Vaagso. They were to clear the area and then move along the coast road and remain as a reserve to Group 2. Group 2 was to attack the town of South Vaagso itself and destroy a number of military and economic objectives, including the canning factory, the power station, the Firda fish-oil factory, and the herring-oil factory. Group 3 was to capture Maaloy Island. Group 4 remained in its landing craft as a floating reserve to be used by Brigadier (now Major-General) J. C. Haydon, D.S.O., O.B.E., Irish Guards, the Military Force Commander, when he thought fit. Group 5 was to be carried on board the destroyer "Oribi" up Ulvesund and landed between the towns of South and North Vaagso to cut communications between them.

Group 1 soon accomplished its task. It cleared the area round Hollevik, captured the village of Halnoesvik, and was ordered to act as reserve to Colonel Durnford-Slater who, with No. 3 Commando, was attacking South Vaagso. On leaving the infantry landing ship, it moved forward in its landing craft with Group 3, which was to attack Maaloy Island, to starboard. It was now half light, and the shore was becoming visible. The roar of the bombardment was loud and continuous; buildings were soon in flames, and it looked to the oncoming Commandos as though the island had been reduced to a shambles. Only a hundred yards from the shore, the agreed signal, a shower of red Very lights, was sent up; the bombardment ceased immediately, and then the Hampdens, which had been circling above, swooped down to 50 feet and dropped their smoke bombs along the edge of the island, rapidly shrouding it in a pall of white smoke, which covered the troops on the last few hundred yards of their journey. To onlookers in the ships, the Hampdens appeared "to float along the air just above the water." They were, in fact, flying at more than 200 miles an hour. All went well save that one Hampden was hit, probably at the moment when her bomb-aimer was about to drop a smoke bomb. The pilot could have turned away and might have been able to alight safely on the sea near the ships. He chose to carry on and fulfil his mission if he could; but the aircraft went out of control, and the bomb fell on an assault landing craft, wounding 20 men. The Hampden fell into the water, and only one of its crew was rescued.

The Commandos Are Hotly Engaged

Group 2 landed very close to the town and quickly silenced two light machine-gun posts. They then advanced into the town itself, where they met considerable opposition. The Germans were by this time fully on the alert, and defended themselves with great resolution in the various buildings in which they were established. Their snipers were particularly effective; they had taken up a position on the hillside west of the town, where they lay protected by excellent natural cover, and caused a number of casualties. While part of Group 2 was thus hotly engaged, another detachment moved a short distance up Ulvesund, landed near the Herring Factory at Mortenes and destroyed it without opposition. In the meantime, No. 5 Group had been taken to their destination up Ulvesund in the destroyer "Oribi." They landed, and subsequently blew craters in the road between North and South Vaagso, and destroyed the telephone exchange at Rodberg.

By ten o'clock the southern part of the town of South Vaagso was in our hands, but the position in its northern part was more difficult. Our advanced troops were held up and had lost their two Troop commanders, Captain Giles and Captain Forester, killed, and three other officers wounded. It was time for reinforcements. They were called for.

While Group 2 was thus involved in heavy fighting, Group 3 had been more fortunate. To the sound of their Commanding Officer, Major Churchill's, bagpipes playing the "March of the Cameron Men," they had landed dry-shod on Maaloy Island. On the way thither, their craft looked to watchers from the air "like tadpoles with white tails moving in perfect formation for the beach." There they found a low rocky cliff, on the top of which they formed up and advanced. The island was thick with the smoke of the shells and smoke bombs. The men advanced to the German barracks, where they killed four Germans and took 25 prisoners, one of whom was the German officer in command, a fat man, the owner of the boots. Of the German guns, all but one had been knocked out. The one gun still serviceable was turned on a German flak ship. During this action, the Norwegian Army Captain Martin Linge, at the head of his unit, made a very vigorous and brave assault on the German Headquarters, and died riddled with machine-gun bullets. He was soon avenged by his men, who threw hand grenades into the building and set it on fire. The island of Maaloy was entirely in our hands by 9.20. About an hour was spent searching it and removing the office files from the German barracks. Soon after 10.30 part of Group 3 were ordered to re-enter their craft and go to the help of their hard-pressed comrades of Group 2 in South Vaagso.

By then the situation there was that small parties, many of them under the command of junior non-commissioned officers, were making very slow progress against stiff German house-to-house opposition. Nor was time on their side; they had to accomplish their task by a fixed hour in order that the time-table for the withdrawal of the Force might not be upset. The reinforcements, however, which they needed had now arrived and the situation was about to change. Half an hour previously, Brigadier Haydon had thrown in the floating reserve, Group 4. They were moving on the north side of the town to the left flank. A few minutes after their arrival, Group 1, which had captured Hollevik without opposition, also arrived and began to drive through the centre of the town and along the waterfront. Not long afterwards part of Group 3 came in from Maaloy Island.

Thus by 11 o'clock four out of the five groups composing the attacking force were concentrated in South Vaagso, bent on the task of overcoming the enemy. Lieutenant-Colonel Durnford-Slater, having dispatched his reinforcements about their allotted task, came forward himself with No. 6 Troop of No. 3 Commando, which had just arrived from Maaloy, and took control of the situation. "His two orderlies," runs the official report, "were both wounded, but with great coolness and complete disregard for personal safety, he reorganised his forces and directed a northward drive through the town until, when he judged the situation to be well in hand, he left Captain Young (in command of No. 6 Troop) in charge and returned to report progress to the flagship." He received the D.S.O.

Shooting It Out in the Streets

Some idea of the nature of this house-to-house fighting can be gained from the account of No. 6 Troop's attack on two warehouses. The second of the two, called the Red Warehouse, was held by a small party of determined Germans, but the first was found to be unoccupied; Captain Young posted two men at a window on the third floor with orders to give covering fire to the rest of the troop when they rushed the Red Warehouse. Between the two warehouses was a small building with a pile of wood beside it; it provided a useful jumping-off place from which to launch the final attack on the Red Warehouse some 60 yards away. No. 6 Troop rushed this building, losing a sergeant killed and one man wounded. A burst of tommy-gun fire through the door produced two Germans, who ran out to surrender. One of them was an opera singer. These were followed by a German sailor and a civilian. The rest of the attack can be told in the words of the man who led it, Captain (afterwards Major) P. Young, who was awarded the M.C.

"I decided to advance immediately to our front and seize the Red Warehouse on the steamship wharf. It was about 60 yards away and, I thought, unoccupied. When, however, I was some ten yards from the door I saw a German soldier standing there, wearing a steel helmet and a long overcoat. I fired at him from the hip, swerved to my left and got down behind a crate standing against the warehouse wall. My men were coming up at the double in the most determined manner; Lance-Sergeant Herbert came first. The Germans threw three stick bombs at us without doing any damage, though one fell within ten yards but did not explode. Our retaliation was to put twelve Mills bombs into the building, mostly through the door. I then ran into the building shouting 'Hände hoch,' thinking that they had been done for; I was immediately shot at from an inner door, returned the fire and came out of the warehouse.

"Lieutenant O'Flaherty and I posted men to cover every window and the door of the warehouse while we reconnoitred it in order to find a way in. The Colonel, however, then came up and told us that we must push on. I decided to burn the place down. We removed three draught horses from the stables where they had been slightly wounded when Lance-Sergeant Connelly flung a grenade into the place on hearing movement in it. We were unable to enter the warehouse from the stables.

"It was while I was organising the job of burning down the warehouse, as opposed to rushing it, that I suddenly saw Lieutenant O'Flaherty and Trooper Sherington dash into the building by the front door. They were both armed with tommy guns. . . . I felt I had to go, too. I was at the bottom of the stairs leading to the second floor, when I heard two shots and both O'Flaherty and Sherington fell. I then fired at the inner door and again withdrew. It was difficult to see how we could rescue them, as they were both lying in the middle of the room covered by the enemy, who could not be seen, for they were standing in the darkness of the inner room not five yards away. Sherington gasped out that he had been shot from the next room.

"It seemed to us that the best thing to do would be to go up the stairs and try to shoot the enemy through the ceiling, though this was obviously going to be difficult. At that moment, however, O'Flaherty and Sherington walked out of the room. Sherington had been hit in the leg and O'Flaherty looked as if he had had a plate of strawberry jam flung in his face. Trooper Hannan caught O'Flaherty as he fell and Lance-Corporal Darts got hold of Sherington. I sent them back to the rear, and dispatched Corporal Chapman of No. 2 Troop to get fire bombs while Trooper Hughes fetched a bucket of petrol. Lance-Sergeant Herbert flung this into the room." A moment later the warehouse was ablaze.

Similar scenes to this were being played throughout the town, as determined men in ones and twos ran stumbling and slithering through snow-covered backyards to burst open the doors of cold, featureless buildings where small bodies of the enemy, with a determination and a tenacity almost equal to that of the Commandos, stood at bay.

8. BATTLE OVER THE FJORDS

The part played by the Royal Navy and the Royal Air Force must now be considered. The Germans did not leave the bombardment of the island of Maaloy unanswered. The battery on Rugsundo was bombed by Hampden aircraft before the bombardment began. Though effective, the bombing did not destroy the battery, which opened fire on the "Kenya" at 8.56 a.m. "While I was looking at the bombardment of Maaloy," says Wing-Commander (now Group-Captain) A. H. Willetts, D.S.O., who led the Hampdens, "I saw what looked like red-hot meteors streaking out from the Rugsundo battery. I could watch the whole length of their flight from the mouth of the gun to the moment when they burst in the sea, when they gave off a cloud of purple smoke." The battery was engaged by the "Kenya" two minutes before 9 a.m. and was silenced two and a half minutes later. The smoke bombs dropped by the Hampdens around the battery undoubtedly played a very effec-tive part in masking it. The Rugsundo battery re-opened fire more than once during the day and hit the "Kenya" twice, a shell holing her above the water-line abreast of the bridge at 1.17 p.m. After that the Rugsundo battery was finally silenced.

At 9.45, the destroyers "Oribi" and "Onslow" passed through the narrow passage between Maaloy Island and South Vaagso and entered Ulvesund. By now it was full day and the scene did not lack majesty. "As the day grew lighter, and the flames and flashes that belong to a raid became less theatrical, steep mushrooms of smoke, some of it oily black and some quite an ordinary bonfire grey, stretched languidly into a very clear sky. An hour or so later, the sun must have topped the crest behind us sufficiently to touch the peaks ahead. They were quite suddenly, quite surprisingly coloured a violent, vivid mauve which spread quickly downwards until it reached the water of the fjord, was gone in a second, and left the slopes brilliant in sunlit snow and deep folds of indigo shadow."

Ahead the destroyers soon sighted two merchant ships and an armed trawler under way steaming northwards. There was also a schuyt of about 2,000 tons. She was anchored close in shore, and as the destroyers passed, the crew waved the Dutch flag, a *ruse de guerre* which succeeded for the moment. The ships were cheered as they moved up the fjord by Norwegian patriots on either side. The merchant ships and the trawler disregarded orders to heave to, and having rounded Brandhaevnes Point they beached themselves, the "Normar" of about 2,200 tons to the south-'ard, the "R. E. Fritzen" of about 3,000 tons in the centre and the armed trawler "Fohn" to the north. Fire was opened upon them, and at 10 o'clock precisely a boarding party left the "Onslow" to board, first the "Fohn" and then the "Fritzen." The German captain of the "Fohn" was a gallant man. On first sighting our destroyers he had rounded up the two other German ships under heavy fire and driven them ahead of him; he also opened fire on our aircraft and may have hit one of them.

The boarding party from the "Onslow" reached the "Fohn," and was at once heavily sniped by a party of the "Fohn's" crew which had gone ashore after the ship had beached. Lieutenant-Commander (now Commander) A. N. P. de Costobadie, D.S.C., R.N., leader of the party, reached the bridge of the "Fohn" where he found the German captain had been killed in the act of throwing over the side his confidential books. The Lieutenant-Commander took up a rifle and opened fire at the enemy from behind the inadequate shelter of a wooden boat. "After some minutes," he said, "the Germans ran from the road. I called to the two seamen with me and we pursued them with shots. . . . I remember laughing at the time for one of the seamen, after I had finished firing, said, 'Had not you better have your tin hat now, sir?' and I found that it had fallen off when I first boarded the ship."

Sub-Lieutenant M. P. Vaux, D.S.C., went ashore with four men and immediately took prisoner 17 merchant seamen. While this was going on, the boarding party turned its attention to the "Fritzen." Here a disappointment met them. Their leader, discovering a fast-shut cupboard in the captain's cabin, blew away the lock with a shot from his revolver, and in doing so broke the three bottles of brandy which the cupboard contained.

The next ship to be boarded was the schuyt called the "Eismeer," which the Germans had tried to disguise as a Dutchman. The boarding party was now under the fire of a very determined and accurate sniper who mortally wounded the stroke oar of the "Onslow's" whaler, and subsequently prevented all attempts to raise the "Eismeer's" anchor. The background of snow and black rock provided ideal concealment for snipers, whose fire was kept down but not silenced by Lewis, pom-pom, Oerlikon and machine-gun fire from the "Onslow." Eventually all three ships were sunk by gunfire from the "Onslow" and the "Oribi," who joined her escort after having taken off 5 Group which had successfully completed its task. They had captured a quisling, received the surrender of the armed trawler's crew and destroyed a telephone exchange.

While these ships were being sunk, a tug and another vessel of about 3,000 tons were seen to enter Ulvesund from the northward. She flashed her name, the "Anita M. Russ," and the "Oribi" replied, thus momentarily deceiving the enemy. She could not send a boarding party because her boats were in-shore taking off 5 Group. Realising what was happening, the tug turned hard aport, the merchantman hard astarboard, and both ran ashore. They were destroyed by gunfire. Some of the German crew were picked up and said that they had at first imagined the destroyers to be German. When asked what they thought when they saw the White Ensign, their Chief Engineer answered for all, "Vi! ve vere ashtoundet." They too, like the rescued crew of the "Krebbs," sunk during the first Lofoten raid, seemed apprehensive of their fate. Their self-confidence was restored when they were given hot drinks and allowed to listen to the Hamburg radio programme on the ship's wireless.

The support provided by our Air Force to the enterprise was of three kinds. Close support, the bombing of the nearest German fighter airfield at Herdla, and a diversion off Stavanger. The part played by the Hampdens has already been described; in addition, Blenheims and Beaufighters provided air cover. A Blenheim was lost shortly after ten in an engagement with two ME. 109's. Ten minutes later two JU. 88's appeared but were driven off by Beaufighters.

Altogether Fighter protection was provided from 9.28 in the morning until 4.15 in the evening by aircraft which had had to fly some 350 miles to reach the scene of fighting. The protection afforded was, on the whole, very successful. No bombs hit the ships. The most serious attack, which developed between 12.30 and 12.45, was driven off by anti-aircraft fire as well as by the fighters. In the air battles which took place, four German Heinkel 111's were destroyed with a loss of two Beaufighters and a Blenheim. Another Blenheim reached base in safety, after hitting the sea and bending a propeller in a fight with an ME. 110; the observer and rear gunner were badly wounded.

The conditions under which air protection was afforded were very severe. The day before, a blizzard had struck the airfields in Northern Scotland from which the aircraft were to operate, so that when the crews came to man them they found four inches of hard-frozen snow on the wings. They chipped it off as best they could with brooms and spades, but many of the aircraft took off with their wings snow-laden. The slip stream gradually blew away the snow.

The assault on Herdla airfield was a most accurate piece of timing. Thirteen Blenheims were ordered to bomb this base, at which German fighters and bombers could re-fuel and re-arm, precisely at noon. Herdla was provided with wooden runways and, if they could be destroyed, the German aircraft would be unable to take off or to land. The bombs struck the runways at one minute past noon precisely, blowing great holes in them into one of which an ME. 109 fell just as it was about to take off, presumably for Vaagso, with the rest of its squadron. A diversion was also arranged and took place off Stavanger, where a squadron of Blenheims attacked enemy shipping with the object, in which it fully succeeded, of occupying the considerable enemy air forces in the area.

By 12.30 p.m. opposition in South Vaagso had almost ceased. For an hour or more before that time, the fjord had been covered with landing craft plying to and fro engaged in the work of ferrying wounded, prisoners and loyal Norwegians to the infantry assault ships. Almost all the military and economic objectives had been destroyed, among them all German offices, the wireless station, a German car and lorry park, four coast-defence guns, one anti-aircraft gun and a tank, an ammunition store, a German barracks, a searchlight and all the huts and houses inhabited by German soldiers. Every other installation of value to the enemy—the lighthouse, the main canning factory in South Vaagso, the herring-oil factory at Mortenes—had been entirely destroyed, while the Firda factory and two other small factories were left blazing from end to end; at least 150 of the enemy had been killed, 98 German prisoners and four quislings had been taken; the number of loyal Norwegians who had accepted a passage to England was 77; nine ships of a total tonnage of nearly 15,000 tons were destroyed. It was time to go.

Small but Significant

The withdrawal took place about 3 p.m. It was almost without incident save for an abortive bombing attack by Heinkels which was broken up by heavy anti-aircraft fire, the bombs falling wide. For an hour our Force was escorted by Beaufighters. During dusk and bright moon-light a single enemy aircraft attempted to attack the Force but without success. It sailed steadily on, while the prisoners were being interrogated below decks and the wounded, of whom there were 71, including pris-oners and Norwegians, were being attended to in the sick bays of the various ships.

So ended the small but significant adventure of Vaagso. The forces engaged were not large, a cruiser and four destroyers of the Royal Navy, between five and six hundred officers and men of the Army and a few squadrons of Hampdens, Blenheims and Beaufighters of the Royal Air Force, but its success was complete. It proved that if adequate Naval and Air support were forthcoming, Special Service Troops could overcome strong opposition and complete their task. The spirits of all who took part in the action were high, and remained so as the day wore on and more and more of the ill-gotten gains of the Germans went up in flames. Only in one heart, perhaps, was there any disappointment. Throughout the action a midshipman was stationed on the bridge of the "Kenya." He had been told that, if she sent a boarding party ashore, he would be in command of it. He waited all day keeping very quiet and well out of the way of his seniors. From time to time he tapped the side of the bridge with a two-foot rod of steel, which he had evidently decided to use as his personal weapon. The hours passed. No orders were given him, and presently his woodpecker tappings ceased. The ships were under way, the adventure was over. He had had a seat in the stalls, but next time he would be on the stage, and then . . .

While the raid on South Vaagso was taking place, No. 12 Commando, under the command of Lieutenant-Colonel S. S. Harrison, M.C., went to the Lofoten Islands, first visited by Special Service Troops on the 4th March previously. Their main object was temporarily to occupy the towns of Reine and Moskenes, and in this they were successful. The infantry assault ship which carried them was camouflaged white, and the Com-mandos wore white overalls and hoods. At 6 a.m. on the 26th December, Reine was reached, the tasks set were accomplished, and a few quislings and some German prisoners were taken. Some of the latter formed the staff of the wireless station at Glaapen. They had not yet recovered from their Christmas festivities, which had included a meal of pork washed down with French wine. The large ration of French chocolate and the 50 cigarettes apiece they had also received had not been consumed, and formed a welcome addition to the meagre rations of the local inhabitants, to whom they were distributed. The Commando was accompanied by some members of the Royal Norwegian Army who were of great assistance. The Force remained for two days, being attacked on the 27th by a German seaplane which dropped a bomb very close to H.M.S. "Arethusa" but without doing her damage. The expedition was successful. The German sea communications in North Norway were interrupted, two wireless stations put out of action and a number of German vessels captured.

9. AN EXPERIMENT IN RADIO-DISLOCATION

On the 1st February, 1942, Flight-Sergeant Cox, an expert radio engineer, arrived at the Air Ministry and shortly found himself in the presence of an Air Commodore, who congratulated him on having volunteered for a special and a dangerous mission. "I cannot yet tell you what it is," said the Air Commodore, "but you must begin by learning all about parachute jumping." Intrigued and obedient, he went away to do so and soon reached the stage when he was allowed to leap from a captive balloon in the middle of the night. "The hole," he says, "in the bottom of the basket, seemed suddenly to me to look like a bottomless pit."

While he was thus engaged, cramming into a few days training which normally takes several weeks, a syndicate at Combined Operations Headquarters was planning a raid of a very different kind from that which had taken place a month earlier at Vaagso.

Like ourselves, the enemy strives unremittingly to improve his system of radio-location. Backward in this at the outbreak of war, by the end of 1941 he had made considerable progress and had established a number of stations on the western seaboard of Europe to give warning of the advent of our bombers. One of these, of the most modern design and construction, was situated near the village of Bruneval, in Northern France, some twelve miles N.N.E. of Le Havre. It was decided to put it out of action, and to use for this purpose men of an Airborne Division, taken to their destination by Whitleys of Bomber Command and brought back to England by the Royal Navy.

The objective, housed in a small cabin standing in a shallow pit, was situated between the edge of the cliff and an isolated house described by Major J. D. Frost, who was the first to enter it, as of "the modern villa type and quite new." A quarter of a mile away to the south, a small steep beach of pebbles and sand lies at the foot of chalk and flint cliffs, more than 300 feet high. It was from this spot that it was decided to embark the force when its task was completed.

The post was manned by German signallers, specialists in the working

of the radio-location apparatus. It was well defended, immediately by a
trench with dug-outs, and a short distance away by a pillbox mounting
machine guns on the edge of the cliff, while another was situated just
south of Bruneval, both covering the cove. Some 400 yards farther
inland was a garrisoned farmhouse, Le Presbytère, surrounded by a
small wood. In all, the area was defended by 15 posts, some of which
faced seawards while others covered approaches to the beach. About a
hundred Germans manned these defences, but not far off was a regiment
of infantry, and a few miles farther on a battalion equipped with
armoured cars. The district was also under the protection of the day
and night fighters of the Luftwaffe.

Careful preparations were made for some weeks before the launching
of the enterprise. Reconnaissance aircraft photographed the objective and
the country surrounding it. From the pictures taken, scale models were
constructed and special maps prepared. These were used to good effect,
for the observers in the Whitley crews were able, after some days' study
of them, to draw from memory accurate pictures of the coast line and the
area of the objective.

All ranks of the three Services rehearsed their parts for some time
before the operation. It was delayed a few days until the weather should
prove suitable. It became so on the 27th-28th February. That night the
weather was at the outset, and for most of the time, perfect. "No wind,
sea or swell and a bright moon with a little cloud and a very light haze,"
reported the commander of the Naval forces. "Visibility in the area was
found to be two to four miles with excellent definition," states the
report of his Royal Air Force colleague. The Naval Force, under Commander F. N. Cook, R.A.N., consisted of motor gunboats of the 14th
Flotilla under the command of Lieutenant-Commander W. G. Everitt,
R.N., assault landing craft and support landing craft, in which were
embarked 32 officers and men of the Royal Fusiliers and the South
Wales Borderers, whose duty it was to cover the withdrawal of the
parachute troops. Two destroyers escorted the Naval forces, which were
the first to move, for it naturally took them much longer than the
Whitleys to reach the neighbourhood of Bruneval. They were far out
to sea by the time the airborne troops took off.

"Come, Sit by My Side if You Love Me"

These, commanded by Major J. D. Frost of the Cameronians, were
over the dropping area soon after midnight. A few minutes before the

time fixed for their take-off they had formed up on the airfield and marched round the perimeter "like guardsmen," with pipes playing. As each section arrived opposite its waiting Whitley it wheeled smartly to the right and entered the aircraft. On crossing the French coast the Whitleys were fired at by anti-aircraft defences and by flak ships. There was no air opposition, for an arranged diversion, carried out by aircraft of Fighter Command, was most effective, and no casualties occurred. The evasive action the Whitleys took, however, put two of them slightly off their course and the troops in them were dropped late and some distance from the point of assembly. This, as it turned out, did no harm, for they came into action later at a most opportune moment.

On the way over some of the men, wrapped in sleeping bags of comforting warmth, sang songs, among them, "Come, sit by my side if you love me," which is the Song of the Parachute Troops, and Flight-Sergeant Cox obliged with a solo rendering of "The Rose of Tralee." Others played cards—the old army game of pontoon. Their spirits were very high: "I can best describe them as terrific," reports Major Frost. Half an hour before they dropped, the leader of the Whitleys, Wing-Commander Pickard, D.S.O., D.F.C., gave the signal, "Prepare for action." The parachutists got out of their sleeping bags and, on receiving the order, went to action stations. The green light shone and one by one they dropped.

"In the moonlight I could see the forming-up place, which was a row of trees by a gully," said Major Frost. "These I saw while I was still in the air. That we arrived just where we wanted to go was in great part due to the excellent air photography, which had been provided when the operation was being planned, and to the model of the country, which every man had studied, so that we all knew exactly what to expect."

The airborne troops landed on ground covered by a foot of snow. "The first thing that struck me," said Flight-Sergeant Cox, "was how quiet everything was and how lonely I felt, and then I heard some rustling and saw something outlined against the snow. It was a container." These containers carried demolition and signalling apparatus and additional arms. The parachute troops equipped themselves with the contents, then formed up in battle formation and moved off to capture the radio-location station about 600 yards away. All carried knives and grenades and a high proportion Sten guns and .45 automatic pistols. The assault party was divided into three. Some, under Major Frost, were to attack the isolated house nearby, in which it was conjectured the reserve crews of the station and some of the crew on watch would be found; others, under Lieutenant Curtis, were to capture the post itself, and the third group were to act as a covering party, taking up a position between the large farm called Le Presbytère and the objective on the cliffs. Another party was to occupy the beach from which all were to be embarked when the operation was completed.

"Hände Hoch!"

Major Frost and Lieutenant Curtis led their men at the double towards the isolated house and the radio-location post. Both were reached in ten minutes and surrounded. The door of the house was open. Major Frost, blowing a large blast on his whistle, rushed in, his men at his heels. They occupied the four rooms on the ground floor. They were empty and clear of furniture. He then ran up the stairs with four men, shouting "Surrender!" and "Hände hoch!" A German, the only one present, was killed defending one of the upstairs rooms. Leaving 12 men to hold the house, Major Frost ran with his batman to the radio-location post, from which the sound of explosions had been heard. He found it in the hands of Lieutenant Curtis and his men, who had bombed the dug-outs and killed five out of the six Germans discovered there. The survivor fell over the cliff, but landed on a ledge about ten feet down and was pulled back. Interrogated on the spot, he told Major Frost that the German troops in the immediate neighbourhood did not number more than a hundred.

By this time they had come into action, and our men found themselves under machine-gun fire from Le Presbytère. Major Frost got his men out of the house, suffering one casualty, and formed them up with Lieutenant Curtis' men and the covering party, to defend the radio-location post, which was now being dealt with by Flight-Sergeant Cox and the Royal Engineers of the airborne troops under Lieutenant Vernon. While they were carrying out their task the German fire, coming from two machine guns resolutely served, increased; two bullets struck a part of the apparatus under Flight-Sergeant Cox's hands. The lights of three vehicles were seen in the distance, moving along the road leading to Le Presbytère.

It seemed that the enemy were about to be reinforced; and Major Frost, having ascertained that the engineers had finished their task, began his pre-arranged withdrawal towards the beach near Bruneval village about 600 yards to his south. The beach is at one end of a road running to Bruneval between cliffs on which there were machine-gun posts. "We knew beforehand," says Major Frost, "that there was a German strongpoint on the shoulder of the cliff where the ground sloped down steeply towards the beach. We suspected that it was not manned. As we reached it, a voice from the beach shouted, 'The boats are here. It's all right. Come on down.'"

They were about to do so when a machine gun opened fire on them from a point on the other side of the gap at the bottom of which runs the road with the beach at its end. There were two casualties, one of them being Sergeant-Major Strachan, who was hit by several bullets, of which three entered his abdomen. He survived the wounds they caused and was back on duty within a few weeks. The retreating parachute troops at first thought that the hail from the beach was genuine, and were about to descend the steep slope to reach it when Lieutenant Ross, who was in command of the party detailed to capture the beach, shouted, "Don't come down. The beach has not yet been taken." Major Frost and his men, therefore, at once took up positions near the empty strongpoint, and made ready to defend themselves against attack from the land.

What had happened was that only about half the party which was to capture the beach had as yet arrived to do so. The others had been dropped two and a half miles away from the assembly point and were in consequence late. There were not enough men to begin the attack without them. Realising this, Major Frost sent ten of his own men to reinforce the attacking party. As they moved off to do so, the missing sections arrived, some of them stout Highlanders, shouting their war cry, "Caber Feigh!" * The attack was at once launched and was completely successful. The garrison of a pillbox were all killed by grenades.

In a small house on the edge of the beach a solitary German telephone orderly was captured. He had stayed there on duty by his instrument, being rung up every few minutes by a Major of the headquarters of the local German garrison who seemed, so the prisoner said, to be in the last stages of agitation and cursed him for making so much noise. The orderly explained that the din was caused by grenades exploding in the room. At that moment the assaulting party burst in and the German surrendered. Another was captured, wounded, in an empty pillbox nearby. These, together with the man taken on the edge of the cliff, were the only prisoners to fall into our hands.

---

* The Antlers of the Deer.

The Boats Came In

As soon as the beach was mastered, immediate efforts were made to get into touch with the landing craft, which were to embark the troops. About 2.30 a.m. their crews saw the flashes of explosive and tracer bullets in the neighbourhood of the beach and made ready to come in to land. They had been waiting for some time, during which they saw two enemy destroyers and two R. or E. boats, which passed within a mile but did not see them. At 2.35 a.m. a signal was received asking them to come at once. The assault landing craft, covered by the support landing craft, immediately put in to the moonlit beach. "The first I knew of their presence," says Major Frost, "was when someone shouted, 'Sir, the boats are coming in.'" The sappers, prisoners and wounded were the first to be put on board. At that moment the Germans manning the cliff defences opened a heavy fire, to which the support landing craft replied with vigour, silencing the enemy. The noise of this firing was very great and the naval officer in charge had to use a megaphone to make his orders audible in the din. All, with the exception of eight, were taken off. Of those left behind, one was dead and the remainder had not yet reached the beach. Our total casualties were one killed, seven wounded, and seven missing.

The Flotilla then made for England. When day dawned it was given air cover by Spitfires of Fighter Command and suffered no attacks from the air or the sea, though at first light it was not more than 15 miles from the French coast.

So ended the operation of which the success was due not only to the valour of the troops, but once more to careful planning and to the close co-operation of all three Services.

10. ASSAULT FROM THE SEA: ST. NAZAIRE

Only Brest and Lorient can rival the importance of St. Nazaire as a German naval base for enemy forces engaged in the Battle of the Atlantic. St. Nazaire contains not only every kind of facility for the maintenance, arming, provisioning and repair of U-boats, but also the only dry dock on the Atlantic seaboard capable of holding the battle-ship "Tirpitz." It was towards this great dry-dock, called by some the Forme Ecluse, by others the Forme Louis Joubert, which is over 1,100 feet long, that the "Bismarck" was undoubtedly making when she was sunk on the 27th May, 1941. If her sister ship, the "Tirpitz," were to replace her in the Atlantic battle, she would, on return from her cruise, have to make use of the Forme Ecluse, or else find her way to the German North Sea bases to undergo the necessary refitting.

St. Nazaire, with a population of 50,000, is by the most direct route over 250 miles away from the nearest British port. It is situated on the right or north bank of the Loire, six miles in from the river mouth which is itself six miles wide, and it is shaped like the letter "L" reversed —the town representing the horizontal and the port the vertical, pointing due north. The port consists of an outer harbour or Avant Port, formed by two jetties and two docks in a straight line. The outer dock, or Bassin de St. Nazaire, is connected with the Avant Port by the South Lock which renders the docks free from tides, and the inner and larger dock or Bassin de Penhouet, with the Bassin de St. Nazaire, by a narrow passage over which is a swing bridge. Ships up to 10,000 tons can enter the Bassin de Penhouet through the South Lock. There is also an East Lock gate lying about half-way along the Bassin de St. Nazaire, reached through a narrow channel which is known as the Old Entrance and which was to play an important part in the operation.

Directly opposite the Old Entrance on the far side of the Bassin de St. Nazaire are the massive submarine pens—nine completed and five under construction. The great Forme Ecluse lies at the south-east corner of the Bassin de Penhouet and emerges beside the mouth of the Old

Entrance at an angle of about 45 degrees to it. Jutting out into the Loire, about half-way between the jetty of the Avant Port and the lock gate of the Forme Ecluse, is the Old Mole, rising 25 feet from the water and providing the enemy with a perfect site for two anti-aircraft batteries. The narrow strip of land, sandwiched between the waters of the harbour and of the Loire, with its power stations, pumping machinery and other lock installations, warehouses and the Old Town of St. Nazaire itself, covers no more than one square mile in all and is an area as closely defended as any along the whole western seaboard of German-occupied Europe. It was against these formidable ramparts that one of the most hazardous and successful experiments in the history of combined operations was launched.

The Plan of Attack

From the outset, the plan of the combined assault on St. Nazaire had a more ambitious military objective than any raid previously undertaken. On 12th February, 1942, the "Scharnhorst" and "Gneisenau" made their way through the Channel to northern waters. Six weeks later, in the early hours of Thursday, 28th March, H.M.S. "Campbeltown," emerging from a tornado of enemy fire, discharged her last duty and rammed the lock gates of the Forme Ecluse, thereby preserving St. Nazaire from the "Tirpitz." The strategic balance in the Atlantic had been materially, perhaps decisively, improved.

In the plan as finally agreed upon, it was decided to make the destruction of the lock gates and mechanism of the Forme Ecluse by H.M.S. "Campbeltown" the principal object, while the destruction, first of the smaller South Lock gates and their installation, secondly of other key points such as pumping machinery for the Bassin, and thirdly of any accessible U-boats and shipping, were to be subsidiary objects in that order of priority.

The Naval Force consisted of H.M.S. "Campbeltown," which was the former American destroyer U.S.S. "Buchanan" put into commission with the Royal Navy, two escorting Hunt class destroyers, H.M.S. "Atherstone" and H.M.S. "Tynedale," a motor gunboat, a motor torpedo boat and a number of motor launches, four of which carried torpedoes and the remainder the Military Force consisting of 44 officers and 224 other ranks of No. 2 Commando and detachments from others. The Naval Force Commander selected was Commander R. E. D. Ryder, R.N., in peacetime an Antarctic explorer and winner of the Polar Medal, while the Military Force Commander was Lieutenant-Colonel A. C. Newman, the Essex Regiment, commanding No. 2 Commando.

Surprise was the essential ingredient in the success of the plan, and elaborate precautions were taken to secure it. A diversionary bombing attack was arranged, the purpose of which was to distract the attention of the defenders' guns from the oncoming Naval Force, not only by bombs but also by the din of the aircraft overhead which, it was hoped, would drown the noise of the ships' engines. Aircraft of Coastal and Fighter Commands were detailed to give protection to the Force on the outward and return journeys.

The military plan of attack was based on landings at three places, over the bows of the "Campbeltown," from motor launches berthed either side of the Old Entrance, and on the north side of the Old Mole. The Force was divided into three main groups covering areas within a convenient radius of these landing points. Each group was in its turn subdivided and given particular objectives to attack and destroy. To each objective was assigned a demolition and a protection party, and it was laid down clearly that the demolition parties were to avoid being distracted from their vital tasks and to leave whatever fighting there might be as far as possible to the protecting parties. With the successful completion of the demolition work, in particular the blowing-up of the bridges which was designed to convert the dock area into an island and thwart any effective enemy concentration, the plan for withdrawal was a systematic convergence on the Old Mole. Two hours was the maximum time allowed for the Military Force to complete its operation, by which time the Naval Force would have to leave in order to get clear before daybreak and regain the escorting destroyers.

It was agreed by the Force Commanders that the "Campbeltown," which was to be under the command of Lieutenant-Commander S. H. Beattie, R.N., being the main unit, should have prime consideration in all matters, and that the light craft should lead her in and give her full supporting fire. Cruising and assault orders were worked out which allowed for any sacrifice in order that the "Campbeltown" might get through. An elaborate system of time fuses was arranged in the "Campbeltown," which made possible the blowing-up of five tons of explosives after allowing first for her impact with the lock and then for her scuttling. This task was entrusted to Lieutenant H. T. Tibbetts, R.N., who was awarded the D.S.C. for a piece of work which has been described by Commander Ryder as "both original and brilliant" and as covering the Force Commanders "against a whole multitude of circumstances we could not foresee."

The planning staffs at Combined Operations Headquarters gave special attention to the draught of "Campbeltown" and the height of the tides in the St. Nazaire area. To these problems was added the need for a full moon, which limited the possible dates for the operation to about five days. But the most important factor of all was weather— not only for the night of the bombing diversion but also for the whole period of the Force's departure from and return to port. Here the prospects were reasonably good. In the early spring, spells of easterly wind are common in the approaches to the Channel, which meant that, once past Ushant, the Force would be under the lee of the land. The wind brings with it bright sunny weather so that the land becomes warmer than the sea, and this causes sea haze off the west coast of France involving low cloud up to 40 or 50 miles off shore, which descends to patches of fog near land. This was the weather wanted, and as it set in well in advance of the official date of departure and there was a risk of losing the advantages of it, the Force curtailed its training, which had already involved a full-scale dress rehearsal at a British port, and set sail a day earlier than was originally arranged.

Alarms and Excursions

In spite of all the feverish preparations, when at last on the 26th March the expedition crept quietly out of harbour, it was the first time that the whole Force had been in company. It was a fine spring day with a swell coming in on the port quarter. Haze and low-flying fighters helped to cover the ships. Commander Ryder made H.M.S. "Atherstone" his headquarters ship during this phase of the operation. The cruising order was in three columns: the port and starboard columns consisted of the motor launches, and the midships column of the two Hunt class destroyers, "Campbeltown," and the motor torpedo boat in tow.

The camaraderie between the Services is a particularly heartening feature of combined operations. Chief Engine-Room Artificer Howard, R.N., describes the arrival of the troops on the "Campbeltown" "in good health and spirits and eager for the fray." "The ship's company and the Commando troops were soon very good friends," he adds, "and telling tales and singing all sorts of songs." A petty officer gave everyone the details of the job in hand, telling them at the same time how to make themselves interchangeable in their duties should the need arise. "We

sat about gossiping," says Lieutenant D. M. C. Curtis, R.N.V.R., commanding the motor gunboat; "it was almost like a pleasure party. When
night fell it was very beautiful. The moon was somewhat misty. We
carried on through the night."

The morning of the 27th dawned bright and clear with visibility now
extreme and the Force in broad Atlantic beyond the range of its air
escort. There was the ever-present danger that it would be spotted by
enemy reconnaissance aircraft and a continuous watch was kept. The
first threat of discovery, however, came from under the sea. At 7.20 a.m.
the "Tynedale" reported an object which seemed to be a submarine
conning tower, and was ordered to investigate.

The first impression was correct. At 4,000 yards the "Tynedale"
opened fire and the submarine crash-dived. A pattern of depth charges
brought her conning tower to the surface and she was probably hit by
gunfire. No more was seen or heard of her, but although her destruction
was highly probable, the result of the action was sufficiently inconclusive
to give Commander Ryder grounds for anxious reflection. "At this stage,"
he reports, "when we were about 100 miles or so south-west of Brest,
I considered that we should continue with the voyage." This decision
was based on the sound opinion that if the enemy had in fact spotted
the Force, he would certainly return to take another look or send aircraft
to attack. With any luck, only the destroyers would have been seen by
the submarine, and so, after keeping him under water for two hours,
the "Tynedale" and the "Atherstone" returned at high speed in a south-
westerly direction, rejoining the rest of the Force by an indirect route.

The action with the submarine was only the prelude to further worries.
Two trawlers, which might well have had enemy aboard, were witnesses
of it. "However," reports Commander Ryder, "they legged it at such
a rate that I felt confident they had not sighted our Force. In spite of
considerable misgivings I decided to leave them alone." After a number
of false alarms the Force was whipped in and cruising order restored
by 11 a.m.

"Don't Forget Whose Father I Am"

By now there was a pall of low cloud which gave good cover from
reconnaissance aircraft. Evasion of French trawlers, however, which soon
appeared from all directions, became increasingly difficult; at about
11.35 a.m. the "Tynedale" was ordered to investigate one which appeared to be coming across her track from the north, while at about

mid-day, the motor gunboat was dispatched to another sighted fine on the starboard bow of the "Campbeltown." Both trawlers were boarded and, after the crews together with charts and papers had been taken off, sunk by gunfire. The captain of one of them was about thirty-three years old; "he was a good type, and my apologies more than once expressed for sinking his ship were met with the reply, 'C'est la guerre.' "

The afternoon was uneventful, and Commander Ryder was able to get some sleep. The force was well up to its scheduled time, and was in a position to proceed during the daylight hours at no more than eight knots, which greatly reduced its chance of being seen. During these hours of tense expectancy, personal comforts were not forgotten. "Our principal food," Lieutenant Curtis recalls, "through that day was large quantities of raisins which I had put in saucers on the bridge —we helped ourselves whenever we felt hungry." "I was even better off," reports Lieutenant K. Horlock, R.N.V.R., commanding M.L.13, "for there was a fine ham on board which was kept in the wardroom. Whenever any of us were hungry (I had by then seven officers on board) we would go down and cut a slice of ham. It lasted throughout the operation."

Just after 5 p.m., a signal was received from the Commander-in-Chief, Plymouth, confirming the existence of five enemy torpedo-boats (each roughly equivalent in fire power to a British destroyer) and giving warning that they might be encountered. Two hours later came the welcome news that two additional escorting Hunt class destroyers, the "Cleveland" and the "Brocklesby," were being sent at maximum speed as reinforcements. When evening came, there was still no sign of an attack either from reconnaissance aircraft or from the U-boat. "Our spirits were high," reports Commander Ryder. "It seemed incredible that we could really steam here without being spotted. Anyhow, here we were, it was nearly dark and the sea oily calm." At 8 p.m. the ships were ordered to stop, and according to plan the Force commanders and their staffs transferred to the M.G.B., which hauled out ahead of the Force. Lieutenant Curtis describes how there were cheers when his M.G.B. left the "Atherstone," who signalled, "Don't forget whose father I am." "This moved us, as 'Atherstone' had been our parent ship for a long time and we appreciated the compliment. I was much stirred as I took my M.G.B. to the head of the line." At the same time, the "Campbeltown" slipped the motor torpedo boat which took station astern.

The Right Place at the Right Time

During the afternoon the Force had been taking a decoy course across the bay southwards in the direction of La Pallice and La Rochelle. The "Campbeltown" had now been ordered to steer north-east at 15 knots for St. Nazaire. During the approach stage the small striking force of the motor gunboat and two torpedo-carrying M.L.s was formed ahead, then the "Campbeltown," followed by the remaining M.L.s in two columns, and the motor torpedo boat bringing up the rear. By 11 p.m., after having been at sea 33 hours, the Force was brought by the most brilliant and daring navigation on the part of Lieutenant A. R. Green, R.N., Force Navigation Officer, to exactly the right place at exactly the right time.

The "Atherstone" and the "Tynedale" now parted company and patrolled to seaward with last instructions to proceed at slow speed and avoid detection. Shortly afterwards, the ships could hear passing overhead the welcome drone of our bombers on their way to carry out the preliminary air assault. By midnight, gun flashes were seen in the distance to the north-east. By 12.45 a.m. on the 28th, the northern shore could be dimly discerned. The "Campbeltown" was started on her course and her speed reduced to 11 knots. Commander Ryder says that at this stage their feelings were "very buoyant but suppressed." The M.G.B., with Commander Ryder and Lieutenant-Colonel Newman on the bridge, leading the line, entered the main channel about a mile west of the main entrance to the harbour. The dark shape of a patrol vessel was seen and safely passed, though the sky was lit with a veritable firework display of blue, green and white tracer from the German A.A. guns.

"The Glare of a Disturbed Enemy"

Shortly after the M.G.B. had spotted the arms of the Avant Port, about a mile off, came the first enemy challenge. It was from someone flashing an Aldis lamp, for the searchlights were still concentrating on our bombers. The M.G.B., now travelling at 15 knots, and no more than two cables ahead of "Campbeltown," made reply; but less than five minutes afterwards the enemy was evidently roused, and every available searchlight concentrated on the estuary, floodlighting the entire Force. "Each boat," writes Commander Ryder, "with her silvery white bow and stern wave was clearly visible, with the 'Campbeltown' astern of us rising up above all the others. The glare of a disturbed enemy was on us."

The resources of bluff and distraction were rapidly running out, with the "Campbeltown" still nearly two miles from the lock gate. A few moments later a dozen searchlights caught her. The period of stealth was at an end, all was now sound and fury. No narrative can do justice to the intensity and splendour of the action that was now joined or give full coherence to the events of the utmost violence and confusion crowding in on each other from all sides at once. The steady sequence of the planning room was lost in the turmoil of the battle.

11. THE GLORIOUS RENDEZVOUS OF
H.M.S. "CAMPBELTOWN"

From the frenzy of the next two hours it will only be possible to pick out the most striking incidents and developments. The atmosphere is best recaptured from the accounts of those who came back, and what follows is mostly pieced together from their own words.

First let us follow the "Campbeltown" to the end of her voyage. The searchlights caught her and "the Germans at once opened fire, somewhat ragged to begin with, which the 'Campbeltown' returned. By then she was directly opposite the entrance to the lock gate."

"I saw 'Campbeltown' urging bravely on," writes Lieutenant Horlock who was watching her from his M.L.; "so many searchlights were concentrated on her and the rest of the party that it seemed to me as though I were taking part in a pre-war Aldershot Tattoo. I could see 'Campbeltown's' bridge being rather heavily plastered. The fire was all tracers and coming from port. Some of it looked like very fast-moving rockets and when the shells ricochetted they looked like sudden stars."

As soon as the "Campbeltown" had been fired on and it was obvious the Force had been discovered, all the M.L.s increased speed to 18 knots and opened up a fire sufficiently heavy both to check and confuse the German gunners for nearly a quarter of an hour. Lieutenant Curtis describes how the M.G.B. rushed past the Old Mole at 18 knots and adds, "I could then see that 'Campbeltown' was being hit very frequently, especially on the bridge. Her engine room appeared to be on fire. By this time stuff was going off in every direction and the noise was very great. We saw the entrance to the lock, put our helm to starboard and let 'Campbeltown' go ahead; she was coming fast and shooting hard. She made a straight dive for the lock gates and she had to help her a flood of towards one-and-a-half knots. There was a hell of a crash."

Commander Ryder, who was standing next to Lieutenant Curtis, describes how "she was lost to us in the glow of the searchlights as we circled round to starboard. The next we saw of her was at the moment of her striking the lock gates. There was a grinding crash and the flash of some minor explosion on her foc's'le as she came to rest. We were unable to see the soldiers scrambling ashore, but we could see she remained fast in the gate with all her guns firing hard up the lock." The plan laid down that the "Campbeltown" should hit the lock gate at 1.30 a.m. She hit it at 1.34. The cool precision and daring with which Lieutenant-Commander Beattie and his men carried out this formidable order has rarely been surpassed in the annals of the Navy. Never has a British destroyer been four minutes late for a rendezvous with such glorious and devastating effect.

The deed of the "Campbeltown" is suitably recognised in the Victoria Cross awarded to her Captain, Lieutenant-Commander Beattie. His was the most immediate responsibility for the raid's success or failure. His colleagues have readily conceded the palm to him. It is on record that there was a special parade organised at Lieutenant-Commander Beattie's Prisoners-of-War camp at which the German Commandant read out the citation accompanying the V.C. This stressed that the award was made, not only in recognition of Lieutenant-Commander Beattie's valour, but also of that of the un-named officers and men of a very gallant ship's company, many of whom had not returned. Particularly memorable was the part played by the men in the engine room who, in all the heat and darkness, stoked the furnaces right up to the moment of impact.

With the bows of the "Campbeltown" well and truly jammed in the lock gate, orders were passed to abandon ship. Chief Engine-Room Artificer H. Howard, who had now to take charge of the difficult scuttling operation, has described how, with all the lights in the ship gone and the steam shut off, the task had to be carried out by torch light. "No time could be wasted and I had to get busy opening valves, etc., to flood the ship." Making his way along the upper deck, through flames which were rapidly enveloping the "Campbeltown," he could see the stern settling down. "On reaching the forepart of the ship I found several of my shipmates standing and these I told to follow me, and through the flames on the foc's'le we scrambled down the ladders placed by the Commandos and got on shore. The Commandos were carrying out their duties of demolition." A series of loud explosions in close succession from the area of the Forme Ecluse testified that this part of the combined operation was proceeding without a hitch.

M.L.s in the Thick of It

The M.L.s, however, which had been advancing in two columns astern of the "Campbeltown," had not fared so well. It had been arranged that the starboard column should disembark their troops by the Old Entrance; but the leading M.L. of this flotilla was the first to be hit and was on fire from stem to stern before she could reach her objective. She was beached at the end of the Old Mole. Of the remainder of this flotilla, some succeeded in gaining the Old Entrance and disembarking their troops. The M.L.s in the port column suffered even more heavily—their goal was the north or landward side of the Old Mole, but in the stress of the battle they were diverted to the more exposed south side. Lieutenant T. D. L. Platt, R.N.R., in M.L. 9, was leading the flotilla, and in his resolve to run his craft alongside brought her, in the face of machine-gun fire at point-blank range, to within ten feet of the Mole. Grenades were lobbed into her from the jetty above and within a few moments she was ablaze. In this extremity, Lieutenant Platt did his utmost to rescue survivors, but his efforts would have been to no avail but for the sudden arrival on the scene of M.L. 8 commanded by Lieutenant T. W. Boyd, R.N.V.R.

M.L. 8 had not been assigned to either port or starboard flotillas but had been given a roving commission to torpedo anything that might be found in the harbour. Lieutenant Boyd was, in fact, searching for a 10,000-ton tanker said to be somewhere in the vicinity. Having gone beyond the dock, he turned about and moved towards the Old Mole, successfully engaging with his 3-pounder and Lewis guns two enemy guns on top of a nearby building. He decided to fire his torpedo at the shape of a German destroyer. He then made for the Mole. By now gunfire was all round and all over the ship but missing it by about four feet, and they were more or less continually held by searchlights. Thereupon Boyd reports, "I saw some men in the water and someone shouted, 'M.L. ahoy!' There were three men in the water whom we pulled out." It was then that he saw M.L. 9 "on fire and smoking like hell. I went between him and the Mole, turned, ran my stern into him amidships. There was a lot of smoke coming from him forward and his engine room was on fire. I got five or six wounded soldiers off, two unwounded and four ratings and I took the Captain of the boat, Platt, off. It was the first day of his first command." For their gallantry, Lieutenant Boyd and Lieutenant Platt were both awarded the D.S.O. Lieutenant Platt will not

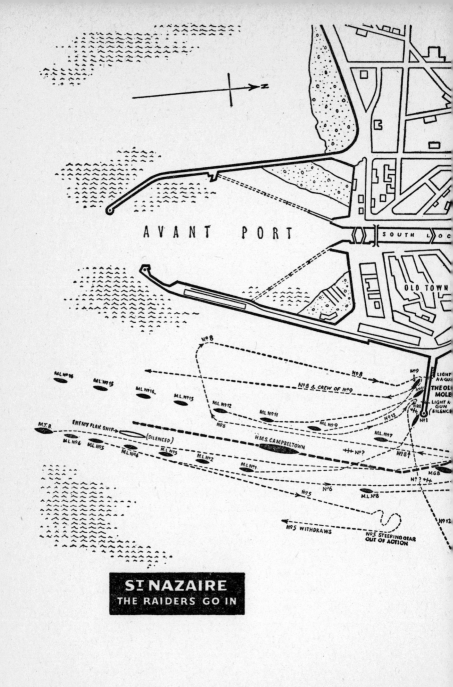

AVANT PORT

SOUTH LO

OLD TOWN

N? 8

N? 8

ML N? 16
ML N? 15
ML N? 14
ML N? 13
ML N? 12
ML N? 11
N? 8 & CREW OF N? 9
N? 9

N? 8
ML N? 9
ML N? 17

M.T.8
ENEMY FLAK SHIP
(SILENCED)
H.M.S. CAMPBELTOWN
+++ N? 7

ML N? 6
ML N? 5
ML N? 4
ML N? 3
ML N? 2
N? 8?

ML N? 1
MGB
N? 7 +++

N? 6
N? 5
ML N? 8
N? 9

LIGHT & A GUN
N? 9
N? 11
THE OLD
MOLE
LIGHT &
GUN
(SILENCE
N? 1
N? 12

N? 5 WITHDRAWS
N? 5 STEERING GEAR
OUT OF ACTION
N? 12

ST NAZAIRE
THE RAIDERS GO IN

300 YARDS 200 100 0 100 200 300 400 500
300 METRES 200 100 0 100 200 300 400 500

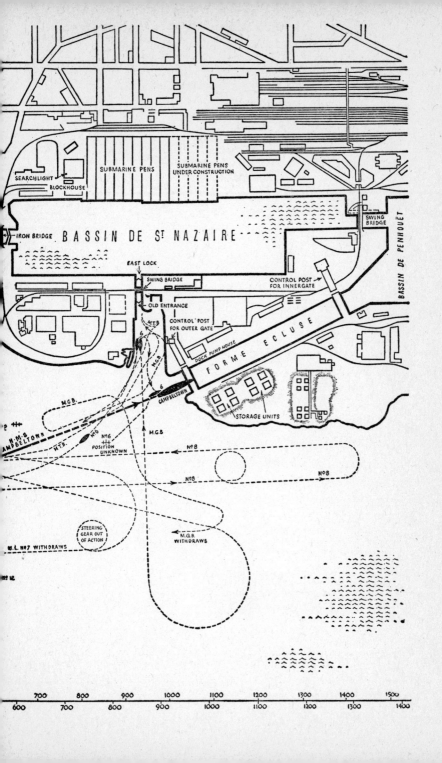

quickly forget his introduction to his first command, and the deeds of M.L. 8 will live to symbolise the daring seamanship of all the little ships in St. Nazaire.

M.L. 6 (Sub-Lieutenant M. F. Rodier, R.N.V.R.), apparently successful in landing her troops in the Old Entrance, was then ordered to take off the crew of "Campbeltown." She made her leaving signal at 2.20, but must have been hit on the way out.

Most of the casualties were heaped round the Old Mole. Lieutenant Horlock in M.L. 13, passed the Mole and then, turning to port in an effort to find out where he was, saw it in silhouette about a mile away. Lieutenant Verity, the Naval Beachmaster, was on the bridge with him. "When we saw it we both laughed. It seemed extraordinary that we had got through all that heavy fire and missed the place." He did not dare to come to a halt as he knew that, if he did, he would at once be hit. As he left he saw two ships to port making out to sea.

M.L. 12 (Lieutenant N. B. Wallis, R.A.N.V.R.), following in the port flotilla, crashed into a boom or rock, and it was this obstruction which, in Lieutenant Horlock's view, prevented all these M.L.s getting close enough to the Mole. Lieutenant Wallis very nearly succeeded in securing a foothold but, with his Oerlikon gun out of action, he could not train his Lewis and Bren guns on the enemy above and was altogether too heavily engaged. Ultimately M.L.s 13 and 12 joined up with M.L. 8— the only three to return to England under their own steam and without escort.

"Like Stitches on a Piece of Cloth"

M.L. 7 (Lieutenant C. S. B. Irwin, R.N.R.) had a roving but extremely hazardous commission similar to that assigned to M.L. 8. She was to move up and down the river twice in each direction at high speed for the purpose of drawing the enemy's fire. Her crew, who were able to get a general perspective of the operation's progress, have related their experiences. In their opinion between 35 and 40 guns were concentrated on the Force. Some of these were undoubtedly mobile, being mounted on lorries or trucks. There was also about the same number of searchlights: about a dozen of these were fixed, of which a few were sighted some distance from the town. They all agree that the searchlights' penetrating power was considerable. Indeed, the light shed by them was so bright that it was easy to read, and even the markings on the Oerlikon shells could be clearly distinguished.

The German machine-gun barrage, they say, was very heavy, about 75 per cent. of it being tracer bullets; the flashes from the tracers as they pounded against the "Campbeltown" seemed to be very much like stitches on a piece of cloth. They described directing their 3-pounder on a searchlight on the port bow which was flooding the "Campbeltown" with light and successfully dowsing it, after which the "Campbeltown" was lost to view, although they were within 200 yards of her. Soon afterwards, M.L. 7 was hit and her steering damaged, but it was repaired again after ten minutes of intense effort. Just when she was turning to go home, she opened fire on a German trawler which was camouflaged with black and grey stripes and silhouetted by a searchlight beam. The trawler replied, setting the M.L.'s engine on fire; "but we fired on his bridge," says one of the ratings, "and quietened him down."

As with the other M.L.s which escaped, they were under intense fire throughout the withdrawal, which, with their engine damaged and making a speed of something less than ten knots, was all the more prolonged and difficult. The ratings of M.L. 7 were deeply impressed by the prompt way in which the Commando troops did their job. It was possible, they say, to follow their progress into the town by the chain of fires which broke out one by one. As one of the ratings put it, "Once they got cracking, they *did* get cracking."

These motor launches—"maids of all work," as they have been called—with no armour, were hardly meant to resist the tornado of metal awaiting them in St. Nazaire. They could achieve total success only with total surprise. The heroism and skill of their crews from the moment the searchlights revealed the little ships cannot be overpraised. It was an experience approaching the limits of human endurance, and they did not fail.

After the crash of the "Campbeltown" hitting the lock gate, the noise continued to be terrific. "I had," says Lieutenant Curtis, "to shout at the top of my lungs the whole time, yet on occasion there would be a sudden lull and then I felt as though I were shouting in a cathedral." The M.G.B., with the Force Commanders still on board, stopped amidstream facing the old lock, and fired at the shore batteries. There was no opposition in the old lock of any kind and two M.L.s went alongside a pontoon on the port side and landed their troops. The M.G.B. followed them, as Lieutenant-Colonel Newman was anxious to take personal command of his troops. The last view of him and his Headquarters Party from the M.G.B. was as they went over the port side "full of beans."

The Landing Parties Get to Work

While Commander Ryder, Lieutenant-Colonel Newman, Lieutenant Curtis and the other officers were on the bridge of the M.G.B. they were all wearing their tin hats. As soon as the firing opened, they automatically ducked their heads as the tracer passed over the bridge. During the height of the action they heard the gunner behind them laughing. "I asked him why," says Lieutenant Curtis, "and he said that it seemed funny to him to see all his officers moving up and down as though they were at physical jerks as the tracer came over. We moved, he said, as one man, very smartly."

"The battle at this moment was beginning to go in our favour," says Commander Ryder. "The weight of supporting fire had evidently been felt, and the Commandos in the area of the 'Tirpitz' dock had undoubtedly overcome the resistance in that area. There was an appreciable slackening in the enemy's fire."

Survivors of the "Campbeltown" were being rushed on board the M.G.B., and Commander Ryder decided to go and make certain for himself that the "Campbeltown" was well embedded in the lock gate. He went ashore; a challenge from a crouching figure with a tommy gun halted him abruptly. "I gave the password, which was my own name, and was permitted to continue. I reached the side of the dock entrance and hailed the 'Campbeltown,' but all seemed quiet there. A small fire was burning still in the fo'c'sle mess deck. The M.L. we had sent alongside her had shoved off and there seemed to be no sign of life. I stepped forward and hailed again, but was greeted by a burst of fire which I imagine came from one of the ships in the dock. It struck the masonry of a small hut close by me. I dodged behind the hut and watched the 'Campbeltown' from behind there for what seemed to be a good five minutes. Then to my relief I saw a series of small explosions along her port side and it sounded as if there were others on the farther side, too. The ship had ridden over the torpedo net and was firmly held by the bows. However, she started to settle by the stern, so I decided that everything was going to plan there.

"My next task was to see how other landings were getting on. As I stood watching the 'Campbeltown,' there was a minor explosion in the big pumping house of the dock nearby. There was a flash inside and the glass flew out of the windows. A moment later, as I was returning to my ship, there was another explosion even nearer, in the hut containing the mechanism for withdrawing the outer lock gate. Apart from this, we heard one explosion farther up towards the other end of the big dock, which I took to be the mechanism for working the other gate, and there was a shed near the pumping house which the Commandos had set on fire. It was now blazing furiously and casting a lurid light on the surrounding buildings and on the black waters of the Loire."

On his return, Commander Ryder ordered Lieutenant R. C. M. V. Wynn, R.N.V.R., in his M.T.B., to go up the lock and torpedo the gates of the submarine base. This order was successfully carried out and Lieutenant Wynn returned to the M.G.B. to report. He had a hurried drink out of a flask with Commander Ryder and Lieutenant Curtis, and after being congratulated by Commander Ryder was instructed to return at once to England. On the way out of the harbour, however, he tried to go to the rescue of a burning M.L., and in the attempt his own ship caught fire.

Miraculous Escape of the M.G.B.

The M.G.B. itself was now an easy target for short-range fire from the Old Mole, which was in enemy hands, and her own fire was largely confined to an exposed fo'c'sle gun. This gun, however, was handled with particular coolness and accuracy by Able Seaman Savage, who succeeded in silencing a troublesome pillbox with it.

The situation was now rapidly deteriorating. They could not see any other craft afloat, and up and down the river there seemed to be several blazing M.L.s. They decided to make a last effort to contact the forces ashore, but there was a fierce battle in progress across the Old Entrance in which the M.G.B., unable to distinguish friend from foe in the dark mêlée, could not safely join. While crouching on the bridge, Commander Ryder held a council of war with Lieutenant Curtis and Lieutenant Green. Theirs was the last ship left; in a few minutes they would be inevitably set on fire like the others. Both the landing places were in enemy hands. "And sadly," writes Lieutenant Curtis, "we realised that there was nothing we could do to help our gallant soldiers on shore." They decided to try to save their wounded and to leave at once. A last signal was made, but it is unlikely that it was picked up on shore.

The escape of the M.G.B. from St. Nazaire harbour was, to quote from the citation accompanying the award of the Victoria Cross to Commander Ryder, "almost a miracle." She was repeatedly hit all down the starboard side, but providentially her engines continued to work, even after the bilge pump of one of them had been shot up. Six Oerlikon shells passed through a petrol tank, but it was full and did not explode. They rushed down the river at 24 knots with searchlight beams full upon them. For 25 minutes they faced this terrific onslaught, all the while the indefatigable Gunner Savage at the pompom maintaining his fire. Commander Ryder and Lieutenant Curtis took alternate turns at the wheel, for the coxswain had been sent down to help the wounded, many of whom had been wounded again.

On board the M.G.B. throughout the action was Mr. Gordon Holman, an accredited correspondent, who, in addition to providing the world with a first-class eye-witness account of the raid, did a splendid job during the height of the action, helping to tend the wounded under the most difficult conditions. He was mentioned in dispatches—a fitting tribute to all the front-line journalists of this war. Among the 14 naval officers to be awarded the D.S.C. for outstanding achievements during the raid were Lieutenant Curtis, Lieutenant Green, the navigation officer, Lieutenant Wallis and Lieutenant Irwin.

Well outside the harbour they saw another M.L. and signalled her to follow, laying a smoke screen to cover her. They were now out of range of the random tracer, only to come under coastal artillery fire of great accuracy. Gradually the searchlights lost them, first from the north bank and then from the south, although the guns continued to fire. Commander Ryder recalls the tragedy of the last salvo of all, "which straddled us in the dark at a range of about four miles, and, to our great sorrow, a splinter struck and killed Able Seaman Savage." For his great gallantry, skill and devotion to duty, Able Seaman Savage was awarded the Victoria Cross, but the citation expressly added that this V.C. was also "in recognition of the valour shown by many other unnamed in M.L.s, M.G.B. and M.T.B. who gallantly carried out their duty in extremely exposed positions against enemy fire at close range."

At about four in the morning, our returning forces which were still fighting their way out to sea observed a tremendous explosion. They assumed wrongly at the time that what they saw was the "Campbeltown" blowing up.

At 6.30 a.m., with visibility about four miles, the five enemy torpedo boats which the Force had eluded the previous day were sighted by one of the escorting destroyers. The "Atherstone" and the "Tynedale" opened fire at the extreme range of seven miles and after ten minutes of desultory action, the enemy altered course away under smoke. Shortly afterwards, the destroyers sighted two M.L.s and the M.G.B. which duly joined up with them. Casualties and military personnel were at once placed aboard the "Atherstone" and the Force set off at the comparatively high speed of 14 knots. Shortly after 9 a.m., the destroyers "Brocklesby" and "Cleveland" arrived and, with their arrival, Commander Ryder, who had already transferred from the M.G.B. to H.M.S. "Atherstone," placed the whole Force, in accordance with naval procedure, under Commander C. B. Sayer, R.N., commanding H.M.S. "Cleveland," who was the Senior Officer present.

Sailor's Return

The return to England was full of perils and anxieties for the now depleted Naval Force. Visibility was extreme and there was the prospect of a lively hue and cry from enemy aircraft as well as from submarines and surface vessels; but although there was, in fact, continuous air activity all the way home, there were very few actual attacks on the Force itself, which suffered no further damage. They were being closely attended by a Junkers 88 when the first British Beaufighter made its welcome appearance. He at once engaged the enemy and, a few seconds later, the Junkers and the Beaufighter successively crashed into the sea. Most eye-witnesses from the ships are agreed that the Beaufighter pilot engaged the enemy so closely that he collided with the Junkers. Various types of German aircraft, ranging from the old Blohm and Voss naval reconnaissance machine, to the latest Heinkel float plane joined in the pursuit to be frequently and effectively driven off by Hudsons and Beaufighters.

During the return, aircraft of Coastal Command made 20 sorties involving 105 flying hours to provide an umbrella for the Force. The danger of bombing was seriously increased by a change of weather. The wind was rising and blowing almost dead ahead and a rough sea was beginning to come up. Under such conditions, the damaged M.L.s were unable to maintain the pace and the Commander, in due course, ordered that the personnel should be transferred to the destroyers and the M.L.s sunk by gunfire. Such decisions are not easily reached and have a special poignancy for the officers and ratings of the abandoned ship. It is reported that one of the M.L. Commanders, who had calmly faced the ordeal in St. Nazaire, burst into tears when the order came that the gallant little ship which had served his crew so well in the heat of battle would have to be sunk in cold blood.

Only three M.L.s, 12 (Lt. N. B. Wallis, R.A.N.V.R.), 13 and 8, completed the course, and they were to find their way home without escort.
Lieutenant Boyd describes how, after the gallant M.L. 8 had been chased
by searchlights and shot up all the way down the river by what he con-
cedes to be extremely accurate German fire, he pursued a southerly
course under the impression that he was being chased by a destroyer.
"I was determined to get home and had decided that, if the worst came
to the worst, we should all go ashore and steal a French fishing boat."
He reached the rendezvous at 5 a.m. and found no one there. Then he
saw some destroyers which opened fire and, mistaking them for Germans, he ordered that his charts should be thrown overboard. On recog-
nising them as Hunt class destroyers he sent a signal requesting that his
wounded be transferred, but there was no reply.

The three M.L.s "stooged around" in these highly dangerous waters
until 10 a.m. when a German aircraft saw them and dropped a stick of
bombs. They then moved west at 14 knots, maintaining that speed until
five in the afternoon. An hour later, there was a second attack from a
Junkers 88 from 1,000 feet. "At 7.30, it came again and flew round and
round us. As it came down to have a closer look, everything opened up.
The first round hit him in the greenhouse and he fell into the sea. A
Blohm and Voss seaplane made a half-hearted attempt to dive-bomb us.
I could see the Lewis-gun tracers hit it and it flew off. Then night fell
and we reached port the next day."

12. "THE COMMANDOS GOT CRACKING"

The story of the St. Nazaire raid is primarily as seen from the decks of the M.L.s. When the Commander-in-Chief, Plymouth, wrote his report on the operation, he was obliged to confess that there was little in it about "the admirable work ashore of the Commando troops because, unfortunately, none who took part has returned nor is there any officer from H.M.S. 'Campbeltown' to give the full story of her gallant exploit." Admittedly, until Lieutenant-Commander Beattie and Lieutenant-Colonel Newman, who are both prisoners of war, can add their personal contributions, the records of this raid must remain seriously incomplete.

Various accounts have come through, on three of which—the most vivid and comprehensive—this account is based. All three authors of them made their escape from St. Nazaire * and joined up with the gallant party led by Lieutenant-Colonel Newman which, with most of its members wounded, its retreat cut off and all available German forces fully roused, resolved to hack its way through the town. We learn from them that the early and most vital stages of the assault were successful. The various parties turned up to report that their primary tasks had been satisfactorily completed. The second phase was one of increased enemy opposition and unexpected trouble in the Old Mole area, which in due course jeopardised the entire withdrawal plan.

One of the authors was aboard the "Campbeltown" on the starboard side, lying down behind the protection shields. "When 'Campbeltown' hit, I was holding on tight and hardly felt the shock." He landed on the road on top of the lock gates but was soon wounded by a hand grenade. He saw, successively, the pump house to port just outside the dry dock blown to pieces, the scuttling charges in "Campbeltown" go up, and a big explosion at the far end of the dock opposite the bow of "Campbeltown."

---

* Their names are not published for reasons of security.

What Happened on the Old Mole

Another of them was with a demolition party detailed to land at the Old Mole in the second M.L. of the port flotilla and to blow up the inner gate of the South Lock joining the outer harbour with the St. Nazaire Bassin. His party consisted of an officer and four N.C.O.s. The landing took place smartly and without any apparent hitch, but the assault party, which was supposed to have landed in advance to make a bridge-head to cover the advance of the demolition party, was not there. Once ashore, they followed some railway lines running along the Mole until they reached some trucks. They were by then under heavy fire, particularly from two machine guns mounted on houses to their left in the Old Town. They tried to take cover behind the trucks, only to find that there was fire coming from a block house on the other side of the lock.

After suffering casualties which included the officer, they were joined by a small covering party consisting of another officer and five men. They decided to try to approach the lock gates by cutting along behind a warehouse and then along the quayside. No sooner had they reached the end of the warehouse than they ran into further heavy fire from the other side of the Bassin, presumably from the submarine pen, and from a ship near it in the Bassin. They had, by now, been ashore for over an hour and the party was somewhat dispersed. One of them was sent on an abortive attempt to contact Headquarters and get reinforcements. Returning from this dangerous mission, he found that the officer had just decided to make a do-or-die effort against the lock gates; but then a runner told them to return at once to the Old Mole, these being Colonel Newman's orders. On their way back, "a bit peeved" at having to leave intact the lock gates they had been sent to destroy, they ran into the Headquarters party near an old house 50 yards or so to the west of the Old Mole. The party consisted of Lieutenant-Colonel Newman, Major Copeland, Captain Day and an assault party of the Liverpool Scottish under Captain Day's command—in all some 50 men, most of them slightly wounded.

"We waited for the M.L.s," the account continues, "and kept a sharp lookout for them, but nothing happened, and I imagined that we had no contact with them. Rumours went about that they had all gone down. We were still feeling quite good; our attitude towards the whole show was that there was a big chance it would be a sticky one, but that we were quite prepared for it. We had been told that if things did become sticky,

we should try to get out of St. Nazaire and make our way back to England
the best way we could. While waiting there, I heard Lieutenant-Colonel
Newman say that we must fight our way into the open country. Hearing
this did not surprise us, because we were expecting him to give that
order. While waiting there he was very cool and made some cracks. I
remember him saying, 'You could do with your ammunition boots now,
couldn't you?' He said this because we were wearing the special rubber
boots issued to us. Our morale at that time was excellent—even better,
I think, than when we were running up and down the warehouse. By
that time we knew what was in front of us."

"Everybody Felt Quite Cool"

Here is another's version of this crisis in the struggle. "Lieutenant-
Colonel Newman recalled us after we had been trying to take the pillbox
for ten minutes. Then everyone was ordered to move back in the direction of the Old Mole with the object of re-embarking at the Old Mole.
By then I understand every party had reported that they had carried out
their different tasks, and there were a good many buildings on fire. I
noticed two, one almost dead ahead and the other farther away and half
right. As we moved forward in single file under cover of the buildings,
we heard a loud explosion somewhere in our rear. By that time, there
was a good deal of fire but none of it was being directed anywhere near
us. As we were moving towards the Old Mole, we passed a corner house
on our right flank, where we found some of the enemy still lying doggo,
who fired at us. On orders from Lieutenant-Colonel Newman, three of
us threw grenades into the house and two men entered with tommy
guns. The house was silent after they came out.

"We then ran down to the quayside and took up positions behind
some trucks in the shadows of buildings, making an all-round defence.
We had hardly done so when we heard a rush of feet and shouts of
'Heil Hitler.' Lieutenant-Colonel Newman bade us hold our fire until
the enemy were 12 yards away; the fire was opened with tommy guns
and Brens. When the fire ceased I heard some moaning and nothing
more. After that a Naval Officer appeared giving the password 'Ryder,'
and I heard him tell Lieutenant-Colonel Newman that the M.L.s had
been sunk and that we had no chance of getting back to England. Everybody felt quite cool on hearing this. In fact, the news was not unexpected because we were convinced, in the ranks, having talked the mat-

ter over, that if the attack was not a surprise our chances of getting away were nil.

"Lieutenant-Colonel Newman then issued the following orders: (*a*) to do our best to get back to England, (*b*) not to surrender until all our ammunition had been used, (*c*) not to surrender at all if we could help it. He then told us that our best chance was to fight our way through the town to the open country. Lieutenant-Colonel Newman was very cool, and made several joking remarks, one of which I remember was, 'It's a lovely moonlight night, isn't it?'"

Lieutenant-Colonel Newman then called together his officers and put the men armed with tommy guns, about 20 in all, in the front. They also had a Bren gun, but the gunner was soon wounded, and it was evident that German troops were concentrating a force in the area to mop them up.

"I noticed Captain Montgomery in the Headquarters party, who had been in charge of other demolition work, and I asked him how he had got on. He said that he had made a good job of the pump house and that he believed the winding gear was also bashed up. As we moved up the side of the warehouse I saw one or two buildings—dock installations I suppose you would call them—blazing merrily."

Some of them discussed whether they should try to swim across the Bassin, for by that time they knew that the lock which had been their original objective was heavily held, as also was the iron bridge next to it.

"Lieutenant-Colonel Newman, Major Copeland and Captain Day were still with us—we soon saw that we should have to run the gauntlet over the iron bridge in the bright moonlight. This we proceeded to do, I being one of the first. We bounded from girder to girder. These girders were a psychological protection, but nothing else, because we could not get behind them." Once they were over the iron bridge, the block house from which the enemy fire had been coming became quiet. One or two then took cover behind a fence and got slightly separated from the rest of the Headquarters party, which was running down a street leading towards the town. While attempting to catch up with Lieutenant-Colonel Newman, they encountered two German S.S. men on motor-cycles armed with light automatics followed by several more on motor-cycles and in a van, who opened fire at long range. "It was a bit annoying but did not cause any casualties. It did, however, give away our presence. We replied to the fire, but we were still doing our best to avoid a major conflict. By then it was about 4 a.m."

"Keep Moving, Lads"

One of the Headquarters party, having also made the successful crossing of the iron bridge, describes running into a large number of the
enemy, whom he took to be German sailors because they were wearing
white trousers. He continues: "The Colonel then shouted to us to 'keep
moving, lads,' so down we went alongside the gardens until we reached
a point where several roads met. Half a dozen of us crossed the open
space where the roads met, making for a street. We reached the middle
of the street, looked round and saw that the remainder of the party
behind us had disappeared."

In this group, which was commanded by a Sergeant-Major, there were
six men in all, but only two of them were unwounded. Typical of the
spirit of these men is the story told of the Sergeant-Major who, with
bullets in his shoulder, arms and legs, came upon a car standing in the
middle of a street with all its lights on. He at once volunteered to start
the car, which they suspected might be a booby trap; but he said, "Well,
if it is, I shall get blown up; if it isn't, we might be able to drive through
the town." He made three or four unsuccessful efforts to start it, but they
could not stay long enough to find out what was wrong. "All six were
still together and all the wounded still fighting."

Meanwhile the main party was still in action. "We worked our way,"
one of them says, "along various streets leading towards the middle of
the town. We were still more or less together and were some 30 or 40
strong. Presently we decided—I think it was Lieutenant-Colonel Newman who gave the order—to try to reach open country via the back
gardens of the houses. We all barged through a house which had no one
in it, though it was clean and furnished. It looked to me like a working-
class house."

It was becoming increasingly obvious that the best thing to do was to
split up into small parties. This was done in accordance with a pre-
arranged plan.

The party, which was already reduced in numbers, was drifting away
in small groups. Eventually two of them, one a regular soldier and
Canadian born, who had recently returned from India, decided to have
a look at the house in the front garden of which they were hiding. They
went in, found some French people and said emphatically, "La porte
arrière!"

"We went through the back door, and they shut it upon us. We heard

Jerry shouting. There was a wall in front of us. It was about ten feet high, and we decided to climb it. There was a pile of logs which helped us up it. We jumped down on the other side into a big garden. Beyond it was a road with Germans moving up and down."

It was now about 5.30 a.m. and beginning to get light, and so it was obvious that they would not be able to reach the open country before daybreak. They decided, therefore, to look for a place in which to hide. They crossed three gardens and reached a house which had an opening in one of its walls at ground level. The opening was about 18 inches high. They lay there for a whole day. It was too uncomfortable to sleep. "From time to time we heard footsteps overhead, and during the day we heard occasional shots and bursts of tommy-gun fire, particularly during the morning. We took this to mean that some of our people were being rounded up.

"There Goes the 'Campbeltown'"

"Between 11 a.m. and noon we heard a terrific explosion. We said to each other, 'There goes the "Campbeltown."' Throughout the day we whispered to each other at intervals and made plans; the gist of our talk was that we must get through. We realised that our greatest difficulty would be to get out of St. Nazaire, and that, to do so, we should have to leave at as late an hour as possible. Our morale was, I think, high.

"About midnight we crawled out of the hole into bright moonlight. It looked like daylight. We thought we had a pretty fair chance of not being spotted. We climbed over the wall into a street, guiding ourselves roughly by means of the stars and the moon. We made our way along various side streets, keeping close in to the houses. We heard some Jerries singing in a house and wanted to go in and empty our pistols into the party but thought we had better not. Soon afterwards we struck the main road out of St. Nazaire. We walked along the side, taking it in turns to lead. We went some two and a half miles along the road, and presently got well out of the town. During this time we did not meet a soul."

The other party had various adventures which included getting caught in a cul-de-sac and breaking out through a German cordon which was closing in on them. They then took refuge in a bombed building, crouching below the level of the ground. After removing the wounded to a nearby cellar in full daylight under the noses of some S.S. guards, they, too, planned to move off in pairs as soon as night fell. Some time during

The spirit of St. Nazaire. *A group of the Special Service troops who went out on the daring and hazardous assault upon the German naval base.*

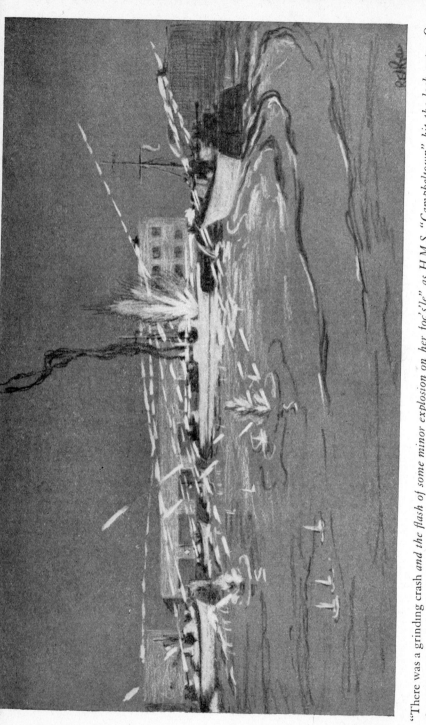

"There was a grinding crash and the flash of some minor explosion on her foc's'le as H.M.S. "Campbeltown" hit the lock gates. On the right (above) is the M.G.B., with the Force Commanders on board, under fire from a flak position on top of a petrol storage depot. Behind the "Campbeltown" can be seen the pump house, later blown up by the landing parties; and beyond her stern is the

"The escape of the M.G.B. was almost a miracle." She is depicted below as, severely damaged, she ran down the Loire at 24 knots with searchlight beams full upon her, under heavy fire from both banks. These two pictures were drawn by Commander Ryder, V.C., in command of the Naval Force.

The great dry dock. *This aerial photograph, taken shortly before the raid, shows two tankers in the Forme Ecluse: the huge lock gate and the pump house on the quay just above it can be clearly seen; also the Old Mole, the submarine pens and the South Lock.*

The dock disabled, showing the caisson, a salvage vessel, a suction dredger, pump house, and outer gate control post.

Ten months later, *the dock still out of action, shows H.M.S. "Campbeltown" halfway down the Forme Ecluse, where the water carried her after the destruction of the lock gates. German engineers have sealed the outer entrance with sand.*
What the "Campbeltown" destroyed. *Photograph of the caisson under construction shows its size and strength.*

Madagascar landing: *Troops of No. 5 Commando leave for Majunga.*

The swift climax of assault. *No. 5 Commando leaps from the landing craft and rushes the open beach of Tamatave.*

Skirmish in the bush. *Commando soldiers move round a hillside for a sharp and decisive attack on a body of Senegalese, established in a village nearby.*

the morning, although they do not remember exactly when, they heard the big explosion. "It was so tremendous that we thought the cellar was going to collapse on us. Everybody said, 'There goes the "Campbeltown."'"

"Between 1800 and 1900 hours," the account continues, "a German sentry walked into the bombed building and peered into the cellar, and said something about '. . . Englander,' from which I took him to mean, 'There are no English here.' He then went away, and the S.S. guards went away too. While he was peering into the cellar, we were crouched ready for him. We could see his boots on the planking on a level with our heads." At dusk, the Sergeant-Major made a reconnaissance, and then decided that they should leave in pairs at half-hour intervals, starting at 2100 hours, and that he and a Sergeant should be the first pair to go. They shook hands and moved off. After that, a Corporal from the demolition party, who felt himself to be too badly wounded to go any farther, went out to give himself up. While he was doing so, another Corporal slipped away on his own; the last two in the party waited for about a quarter of an hour before they also went.

Assessment of Damage

The rest of these men's travels cannot be pursued further here; but they are a tribute to the mental and physical resilience of the men who are trained for special service duties on combined operations. It will be noted that these accounts confirm the evidence of other reliable but secret sources that the "Campbeltown" did not blow up until the morning following the raid; the explosion heard by the returning Naval Force at 4 a.m. must have been the result of some other powerful demolition.

From all the evidence at present available it is clear that the primary purpose of the raid, the destruction of the dry dock together with the pump house and winding gear in the vicinity, was successfully accomplished. Among the subsidiary damage was the sinking of a merchant ship near the inner gate of the South Lock, considerable destruction on the quays, damage to the warehouse behind which he and his party sought shelter, the destruction of gun positions and of a certain amount of German shipping in the Loire, including at least one ship put out of action by the Germans themselves.

Intelligence reports and reconnaissance flights confirm that the outer caisson was lying inside the dry dock badly buckled and forced off its sill. The dry dock was shown to be fully exposed to the sea. For some months the Germans had been reclaiming land in the St. Nazaire area by means of a suction dredger and pipe line discharging sand at the required point. It would seem that the pipe line, after the raid, was extended to the dry dock for the purpose of filling it up with sand and reinforcing the inner caisson. This means, however, that the dock itself is likely to be out of action indefinitely.

It is now known that, at the time the "Campbeltown" blew up, an inspection party of some 40 senior German officers including, probably, the Officer Commanding in the area, were aboard trying to find out how best she could be moved. They were all wiped out by the explosion, together with a great many German soldiers who, as sightseers, were swarming round the part of the dock where the ship lay. The price the Germans paid for their curiosity was a death roll of nearly 400 officers and men. Two days later, both sides of the lock were still littered with human remains which German military working parties, dazed and disorganised, were shovelling together and covering with sand.

Pandemonium Broke Loose

But this was not all. At 4.30 p.m. on Monday, the 30th March, the port area was shaken by another heavy explosion and everyone at work in the port rushed back to the lock to see what had happened. Actually, it was the first of Lieutenant Wynn's delayed-action torpedoes, which had gone off in the Old Entrance lock gate 60 hours after it was discharged. An hour later, a second torpedo shattered the remains of this entrance; then pandemonium broke loose. All the workers in the area rushed to the bridge over the remaining lock gates of the Forme Ecluse. The bridge was jammed with workmen, both French and German, and the exit was barred by sentries. The workmen overpowered them and rushed on to the bridge which crosses the point joining the St. Nazaire and Penhouet basins, throwing their bicycles over the barrier. German sentries opened fire and this was the signal for general firing to break out over the port. No fewer than 280 French workmen were killed in this indiscriminate massacre.

German casualties were heavier still. Having lost most of their officers ashore or aboard in the "Campbeltown" explosion, leaderless German soldiers imagined they saw British Commandos round every corner in the port area. A large number of workmen of the Organisation Todt, who were employed in various jobs, joined in the general mêlée and were mown down by machine guns. Their khaki uniforms were mis-

taken for British battledress. Most of them were killed running across
the railway lines and in the Penhouet neighbourhood as they left work.
Houses facing the Avenue de Penhouet were pock-marked with bullets
and shell holes, and a heavy engagement was evidently fought here
against the imaginary enemy. After dark, the German soldiers kept up
the battle with themselves, returning each other's fire to good effect. In
all, it is estimated that between three and four hundred Organisation-
Todt workmen and soldiers were killed.

The Germans closed the whole harbour area for the remainder of that
week and they evacuated all the population of the Old Town.

The raid on St. Nazaire is the only operation in this war so far for
which three Victoria Crosses have been awarded. "I regard the attack
on St. Nazaire," writes the Commander-in-Chief, Plymouth, in his
remarks on the operation, "as more difficult than that on Zeebrugge, as
a large, weakly-armed Force had to make an undetected passage of over
400 miles to the scene of action at an average speed of eleven and a half
knots through an area usually covered by enemy and air reconnaissances." Having overcome all these preliminary hazards and retained
surprise to the cannon's mouth, the principal object was completely
achieved and most of the demolitions carried out with the utmost speed
and effect.

The Naval losses amounted to 34 officers and 151 ratings killed or
missing out of a total of 62 officers and 291 ratings who sailed from
England. From No. 2 Commando 34 officers and 178 other ranks out of
a total of 44 officers and 224 other ranks were left behind; but the tally
of those who survived and were taken prisoner is high; and, to quote
again from the report of the Commander-in-Chief, Plymouth, "taking
into consideration the extreme vulnerability of the coastal craft, neither
the losses in men nor material can be considered excessive for the results
achieved."

The attack on St. Nazaire showed what contribution could be made
by a combined operation against an enemy base towards winning the
battle of the Atlantic. The manner and method in which it was carried
out proved that it was possible for a comparatively small force to attack
a heavily-defended port under cover of darkness by exploiting to the
full the element of surprise.

German propaganda reactions alone were significant evidence that
the impact of the raid made deep inroads upon enemy morale. There
was the same reckless cross-fire in propaganda, from which emerged

what Mr. Churchill has termed "the dull, low, whining note of fear."
For the French people, St. Nazaire aroused all too easily resistance that
could not be encouraged and hopes that could not be implemented. The
valour of those citizens—including the old lady who told the Prince de
Ligne that she had done her duty despite the weight of the flower-pot—
citizens who, regardless of all personal consequence, joined in the fray
and were rewarded with the full severity of Nazi reprisals, is of itself
no mean incident in the renaissance of France. The attack on Zeebrugge
has been described as "the finest feat of arms" in the 1914-18 war and as
an episode unsurpassed in the records of the Royal Navy. By the inex-
orable standards of history, therefore, the combined operations at St.
Nazaire are already assured of a high place in the scroll of British battle
honours.

13. THE STORMING OF DIEGO SUAREZ

A rapid glance must now be taken at a very different theatre of war, situated thousands of miles from the British Isles, where we are contending against a different but equally tenacious foe. By the Spring of 1942, Japan's successful invasion, first of Malaya, then of the Dutch East Indies, and finally of Burma had radically altered the situation in the Far East. Weakened by the loss of the "Prince of Wales" and the "Repulse," the Royal Navy found itself under the necessity of maintaining strong forces in the Indian Ocean to prevent the further expansion of Japan to the West. Our main route of supply to our armies in the Middle East round the Cape of Good Hope up the east coast of Africa to Suez was threatened. For the Japanese to attack it from bases in Burma was impracticable; the distances were too great. If, however, a good harbour with modern facilities and defences could be seized within striking distance, then our supply line might be cut or at least severely damaged, and one of the main objects of Axis strategy would be gained. Japan and Germany might meet in the shadow of Sinai.

Such a harbour lay ready to hand. The Vichy French Naval Base at Diego Suarez on the northern tip of the island of Madagascar is deep, protected and well fortified. Could it be seized, then raids against our convoys and large-scale operations in the Indian Ocean would become possible. To remain inactive under such a threat would have been suicidal. The Mediterranean route to Egypt was very far from secure. General Rommel was still in the field and was soon to drive back the Eighth Army almost to the gates of Cairo. German and Italian bombers and submarines, with the advantage of numerous bases in Sicily, Tripoli, Southern Italy, Greece and Crete, were making the passage of convoys through the inland sea a most hazardous undertaking. Nothing less than the maintenance of the supply of arms, munitions and every other kind of necessity for the Middle East, Iraq, Persia and Russia was at stake. Once more, as with Syria, we had to turn our armies against friends whose leaders had betrayed them into bondage.

It was realised that opposition might be offered by those whom the Vichy Government had put in command at the time when they had imprisoned all authorities in Madagascar known to be anti-Nazi and favourable to our cause. Leaflets explaining the situation and the motives which had made it imperative for action to be taken had been prepared by us, and it was hoped that the French troops would respond to the arguments they presented. Nevertheless, every military precaution was taken to ensure success. As it turned out the operations which resulted in the capture of Diego Suarez lasted little more than two days. Many of the officers imposed by Vichy fought with determination, sometimes manning machine guns whose crews were unwilling to fire on men who came as their friends. There is little doubt that had the French rank and file shared the zeal of their officers, the operations would have been prolonged and the casualties on both sides far heavier.

An overseas combined operation of this magnitude, which was in fact an invasion followed by an occupation of the invaded territory, is planned and organised by the Service Ministries in consultation with Combined Operations Headquarters. In this particular operation, the air support had, by the nature of the military problem, to be provided by carrier-borne aircraft of the Fleet Air Arm. The Admiralty and the War Office had, therefore, the major share in drawing up the plans, and the expedition was placed under the orders of Rear-Admiral E. N. Syfret, C.B., R.N.

Most of the Royal Naval landing ships and craft that were used to transport the troops, which included No. 5 Commando, and to put them ashore, were provided by the Combined Operations Command. These did not form the majority of the ships and troops taking part. It is impossible, however, to tell the story of No. 5 Commando, which was the Command's land contribution, without giving some account of the land operations as a whole.

The Madagascar operation, in which the Command acted as an assistant and not as a principal, brought out for the first time what has now become one of its most important functions. This is to provide amphibious equipment and specially trained men, and to help generally in making possible the conduct of combined operations on a scale much larger than those involved in raiding the enemy. Another of its functions, equally important, is to arrange special training for the troops who take part in these larger operations and to help stage the final

rehearsals which are carried out before the forces chosen are launched
upon the enemy.

Assault in Three Phases

By March 1942, the long voyage of a Brigade and No. 5 Commando
from the United Kingdom to Madagascar had begun. Two other
Brigades were picked up on the way out.

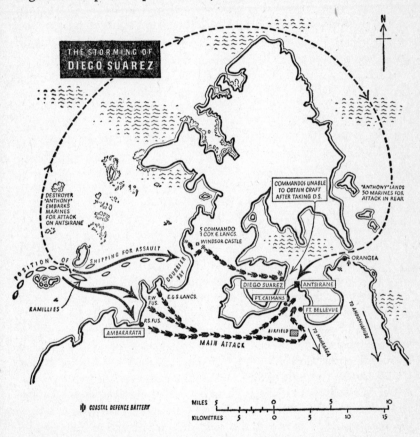

The plan of attack was for a combined assault to be made by an Army
and Naval Force, supported by aircraft of the Fleet Air Arm operating
from H.M.S. "Illustrious" and H.M.S. "Indomitable." They were first
to drop leaflets. If these failed to make it clear that our only reasons for
occupying Diego Suarez were of a strategic nature and directed against

the Japanese, then, and then only, were bombs to be dropped. The targets were to be a number of strategic points, notably the airfield at Antsirane, while a Naval diversion was to be carried out on the east coast of the island. The attack was to comprise three phases. The assault brigade, composed from Royal Welsh Fusiliers, Royal Scots Fusiliers, the East Lancashire Regiment, and the South Lancashire Regiment, was to land on three beaches in Ambararata Bay and advance, supported by tanks, to the capture of Antsirane 21 miles by road to the eastward. No. 5 Commando and a Company of the East Lancashire Regiment were to land farther north at the northern end of Courrier Bay, silence two coast-defence batteries, and then advance eastward to secure the peninsula on which lay the village of Diego Suarez, which is separated from Antsirane by a strip of water some 1,200 yards in width.

These landings were to be followed by that of the support Brigade consisting of the Royal Scots Fusiliers, the Northamptonshire Regiment, and the Seaforth Highlanders, who were to help in the capture of Antsirane and the peninsula to the east of it, on which were mounted coast-defence batteries at Orangea. Together with those at Antsirane, they covered the narrow entrance to the harbour. The Military Force Commander was Major-General R. G. Sturges, C.B., R.M.; Captain G. A. Garnons-Williams, D.S.C., R.N., of the Combined Operations Command was the Naval Commander of the Assault Landing Craft.

At 4.30 on the morning of the 5th May, the assault was opened by No. 5 Commando and the Company of the East Lancashires. They met with no opposition, and at once overcame the only coastal-defence battery found, which was situated at a point called Windsor Castle. Most of its garrison were still in bed and were taken completely by surprise. A number of machine-gun nests, however, held out and were not finally subdued until the afternoon. No. 5 Commando then swept onwards and reached Diego Suarez village, which fell into their hands soon after 4 p.m. Thus the first part of the plan had been accomplished without difficulty in just under 12 hours. The French had not been expecting any attack from Courrier Bay because of the difficult approach to it, which had been mined. The mines, however, were swept, and in carrying out the landings the Royal Navy showed skill and seamanship of a very high order.

In the meantime the main landings had taken place on three beaches at Ambararata Bay. Opposition was slight except on one beach where 50 Senegalese troops were surprised and captured. The great difficulty, however, lay in getting ashore the armoured vehicles, including the tanks. There was a considerable swell and many of them were swamped and had to be hauled ashore. This resulted in a large number of mechanical breakdowns during the operations of the first day.

An hour after the Commando had made its landing, the arranged diversion began. The Fleet Air Arm bombed the airfield six miles to the south of Antsirane and shipping in the harbour. There is no doubt of the success of these attacks, for after their delivery the garrison had almost no aircraft serviceable with which to carry out reconnaissance. The naval diversion was begun at twenty minutes to five by the firing of star and smoke shells at Ambodivahibe Bay, south-east of Antsirane, the most likely landing place on the east coast.

Advance to Antsirane

As soon as they had secured their beaches, the assault Brigade advanced east along the single road to Antsirane. After a time, they were preceded by Bren-gun carriers, which came under fire by eleven o'clock from a position held in some strength. It was attacked by two companies of infantry supported by howitzers and three tanks. Once these had broken through, the fire ceased. Again, so great had been the surprise that the position had only been half manned.

Soon after three in the afternoon the advance was continued towards Antsirane, the tanks leading the way. They destroyed two detachments of lorry-borne reinforcements; but when they reached the main posts of the Vichy French Forces, they came under the fire of concealed French Seventy-Fives, and were held up by this and by an anti-tank ditch. The infantry came up, but could do little; when night fell with tropical suddenness at 6.30, they were still under heavy fire and not able to advance. They had reached the position about 5 p.m., having left their infantry landing ships at 1.30 in the morning and marched some 18 miles from the beaches in tropical heat along a bad and very dusty road. They had had to take with them all their weapons and drag their ammunition and stores in hand-carts.

It became clear that the main positions would have to be stormed by an attack carried out by at least a Brigade. They faced south across the narrowest part of the Isthmus of Antsirane and consisted of a trench system 2,000 yards long, ending to the west in Fort Caimans and to the east in Fort Bellevue. In front was an anti-tank ditch, and on each flank steep slopes covered with scrub ran down to join the mangrove swamp

bordering the sea. The roads running through the position were protected by concrete pillboxes mounting Seventy-Fives and machine guns.
It was decided to attack at dawn.

In the rear many difficulties were still being caused to the crews of the
landing craft by the heavy swell. It was possible to land vehicles and
stores only on one beach instead of on three. The presence of mines kept
the ships from coming near in to shore, and a strong wind slowed up the
blunt-nosed craft as they ran in and drenched all on board with spray.
Though all the men composing the assault Brigade were ashore by
eleven o'clock in the morning, the last of their vehicles was not landed
until midnight. The support Brigade began to land at 11.15 and went
on doing so without a halt except during the hours of darkness, from
6.30 until 10.30, when the moon rose. A brief respite was necessary, for
crews of the landing craft working under such uneasy and troublesome
conditions had become exhausted. A battery of howitzers was landed
in Courrier Bay, the gunners working at times up to their necks in
water to get the guns ashore. They eventually came into action and
shelled the Antsirane defences.

As planned, the attack on the main position was launched at dawn on
a three-battalion front. The South Lancashires on the right penetrated
the very difficult country lying between Fort Bellevue and the sea, out-
flanked the position and captured several hundred prisoners. Their wireless sets, however, were not working, and the extent of their success was
not therefore known to General Sturges at British Headquarters. Indeed, having no news, he thought that most of the South Lancashires
had been killed or captured. Had he been in possession of the true facts,
the reserve Battalion could have been used to exploit this initial success
and Antsirane might well have been captured that morning. The remaining Battalions—the Royal Scots Fusiliers in the centre, and the East
Lancashires on the left—made a frontal attack, but on reaching the
exposed ground immediately before the enemy's position, were held up
by heavy fire and incurred a number of casualties, which grew steadily
until they were forced to retire.

Artillery Duels in the Bush

Observation for the guns was very difficult, for shell fire soon set alight
the bush and clouds of smoke and flame obscured the vision. The enemy's guns were well sited, and it was presently realised that it would be
quite impossible to knock them out with the four 3.7-in. howitzers and

the two 25-pounder field guns which was all our artillery then in action. The assault brigade sat down to wait for the support brigade. On its arrival it was decided to make a night assault beginning at 8.30 p.m., and preceded by an artillery and air bombardment. As a diversion, 50 Royal Marines were to be put on board the destroyer H.M.S. "Anthony" and run into the harbour of Antsirane, where they were to land on the jetty and make a direct assault on the town from the rear. During the remainder of the day our aircraft made a large number of attacks with bombs and machine-gun fire on the main position, which was also shelled by artillery and by the destroyers.

At 8.30 p.m. a Battalion of the Northamptons and a Battalion of the Seaforths, strengthened by one Company of the Royal Welsh Fusiliers, began their advance. They had about three-quarters of a mile to go before reaching the French lines. They pressed on for 600 yards, and passed between the two forts undetected. They penetrated some 1,800 yards beyond the tank ditch and the trench system, and at 11 p.m. sent up rockets announcing their success. The rest of the brigade went forward, pressed through to the town of Antsirane, and presently reached the main harbour without serious opposition. By one o'clock in the morning the Residency had been entered and the town had fallen.

The Dash of the Royal Marines

Its fall was largely due to the gallant action of the 50 Royal Marines who had been detailed to create a diversion. They came from H.M.S. "Ramillies" in Courrier Bay, and were trans-shipped into the destroyer "Anthony," which at once made off at high speed for Antsirane Harbour. The "Anthony" entered it at eight o'clock in pitch darkness, under the fire of every gun that could be brought to bear on her. This fire she returned, and shot out the only searchlight turned on her. She ran alongside the wharf, the Marines tumbled over her stern and were ashore. Their orders were to attack everything except the barracks and the magazine, which were known to be strongly held, but within half-an-hour they were in possession of both of them. They accomplished this dashing attack with but one casualty, and there is little doubt that their swift action prevented heavy street fighting, which would have caused many casualties and much damage to the town itself. In a subsequent official report, these 50 sea-soldiers are described as having created a "disturbance in the town out of all proportion to their numbers."

All resistance had by now ceased in the town, but Fort Caimans and

Fort Bellevue held out until 2 p.m. on the next day, the 7th May, when they surrendered. During that afternoon the Orangea peninsula with its coast-defence guns also surrendered and was occupied on the next day. Thus in less than three days the great harbour of Diego Suarez was in our hands at a cost of about 500 casualties—less than one-sixth of them being fatal.

At times the French fought well; but there is little doubt that the surprise of the attack disconcerted the garrison, especially those whose heart was not altogether in the fight.

Subsequently it became necessary to extend our control over the whole island of Madagascar. In the operation involved, No. 5 Commando and the crews of the landing craft of Combined Operations Command continued to play their part. At one moment during the attack on Tananarive the crews in question had to land the men and stores for two Brigades with only fifteen landing craft at their disposal. With the additional aid of five small captured tugs and eleven lighters this task was successfully accomplished. At another moment, during the attack on Majunga on the west coast of the island, though the assault troops met with little opposition on the beaches or in the town, the naval personnel were subsequently faced with heavy sniping, which delayed the boarding and anti-sabotage operations. This was subsequently put an end to by the Naval Beach Commando, who used their Lewis guns and grenades to good effect.

During operations on land, 58 bridges were repaired and the crews of the landing craft and beach parties successfully coped with the big break in the line of communications to Brickaville by running a rope ferry across 300 yards of river. Two lighters were then brought up to ferry engines across, and a light railway was laid from Tanpani through 50 miles of lagoon and river to Brickaville. "Our dredger was a priceless business," reports Captain Garnons-Williams; "twelve Malgaches with long shovels were put on board a tug and hopped over the side to dig a passage for the engine when the shoal water was reached."

No. 5 Commando made a landing at Majunga, which they captured in less than an hour, after overcoming opposition from French officers who served some of the machine-gun defences with determination and gallantry. One Troop assisted this operation by carrying out a successful diversion on the coast of Morondava. A few days later Tamatave was taken by the Commando.

The operations, which resulted in the occupation of Madagascar, were eventually completed at midnight on the 5th/6th November, 1942. The resistance, to quote the Prime Minister, had been "mainly symbolic." The Combined Operations Command is proud to have had its share in them but the chief credit for their success must go to the main forces of the Royal Navy and the Army who carried them through with resolution, despatch and a minimum of casualties.

14. RECONNAISSANCE IN FORCE: DIEPPE

The raid on Bruneval had been small, short and sharp; its success had been complete. The raid on St. Nazaire had been larger, longer and sharper; its success, measured in terms of the Battle of the Atlantic, also complete. It was time to plan the next stage.

In the spring of 1942, the demands of other and distant theatres of war still prevented the concentration in England of a United Nations force large enough and sufficiently well trained and equipped to launch a full-scale invasion of German-occupied Europe. Moreover, to transport thither a force of this size, and to keep it supplied, would require a quantity of shipping in excess of what it was then possible to collect if the widespread commitments of the United Nations throughout five continents were to be adequately met. What could be done was to raid Europe in force. To mount a raid on a much larger scale than that which had been carried out on St. Nazaire would not only harass the enemy, which is, it cannot be too often repeated, the primary object of raiding; it would also be a means of providing the Allied General Staffs with very important and, indeed, essential information concerning his defences in the West. His strength must be tested, his methods examined at the point of the bayonet and the Bren gun, if the military problem which the forces of the United Nations will have to meet, should it be decided to launch an army of invasion across the narrow seas, is to be solved.

The task was hazardous, but then so is any operation of war, and the end was imperative. Plans, therefore, for a large-scale raid against a point on the French coast, were under discussion early in April, less than three weeks after the raid on St. Nazaire. It was decided that Dieppe was a suitable objective for an operation of the size contemplated. It was chosen from a number of French ports, all equally well defended, as could be seen from the study of air photographs. The Dieppe defences could therefore be taken as a fair sample of what the attackers might have to meet at whatever point an assault was launched along the coast of

Northern France. Among other reasons for this choice, many of which
must remain secret for the present, were several which should be
obvious. Dieppe possesses a harbour used by the enemy as a port of call
for his coastwise convoys, on which he is compelled to rely to an ever-
increasing extent for supplying his far-flung garrisons. To render the port
unusable would be to hamper the movements of such convoys. There
are also in Dieppe marshalling yards, gas works, a power station, petrol
dumps and a pharmaceutical factory, all of which it was desirable to
destroy.

Moreover, an attack by surface forces in broad daylight against territory regarded by the enemy as his own would, it was thought, provoke
the Luftwaffe into giving battle on a really extensive scale, whereas mere
air action by itself had repeatedly failed to produce such a battle during
the previous months. This was eminently desirable at a time when so
much of the German Air Force was concentrated against our Russian
allies. Heavy losses over France might well compel Göring to switch
bombers and fighters from the East to the West.

Natural Obstacles and Coastal Defences

The planners were at once confronted with two difficulties, the first
provided by Nature, the second by man. Not inaptly has that stretch of
France's seaboard running roughly from Cape Gris Nez in the north
to the mouth of the River Saane, a few miles south-west of Dieppe, been
called "The Iron Coast." Nearly all of it is made up of high cliffs,
mostly unscalable, broken here and there by narrow clefts or by the
mouths of rivers. The chief of these is the Arques, on which the town and
harbour of Dieppe are built. Here the gap is something above a mile
in width. At the foot of the cliffs lie stony and inhospitable beaches,
the haunt of picnic parties and bathers in peacetime during the summer
months. To land at low water on these beaches is very difficult and
dangerous because of the rocks in the sea's bed and the angle of the
shore itself, which make the task of beaching a landing craft and taking
it away a matter of the greatest skill and judgment. The clefts behind
the beaches are not numerous and those which exist are, for the most
part, narrow and very easily defended. Men moving up them to the
attack are at the mercy of defenders in position at their top, who can
destroy the attackers with the greatest ease as they clamber laboriously
upwards.

To the natural obstacles of such a coast, the Germans have added

defences disposed so as to cover, with a formidable fire of all arms from
5.9 coast-defence guns to rifles, every likely landing place, especially the
main beach running parallel to the Dieppe promenade. Not only this,
but many of the defences have been designed to prevent ships from
coming close in shore and certainly from remaining there. The planners,
therefore, came to the conclusion that naval support to the land forces
attacking Dieppe—an indispensable adjunct of success—could only be
provided if two heavy coast-defence batteries, one at Berneval on the
east and the other at Varengeville-sur-Mer on the west of Dieppe, were
first subdued. Their fire would do too much damage to ships to make
a daylight attack a feasible proposition. Nelson's dictum that "three guns
in a well-constructed battery, properly placed, would beat off or destroy
any ship in the world" was in their minds when they determined that
the destruction of these batteries was a *sine quâ non*. The planners
worked steadily on, and in due course the Outline Plan for the assault
was submitted to the Chiefs of Staff Committee and approved by them.

The Canadians, supplemented by Commandos, were chosen for the
main part of this hazardous and honourable task. Many of them had been
under arms for three years. They had come to Europe in the expectation
of fighting in France with the B.E.F. But their time had been spent
practising the evolutions of modern war in the quiet fields of southern
England where, soon after they arrived, they had expected to fight a
savage battle of defence. Each and all of them were filled with an intense
and forcibly-expressed desire to come face to face with the enemy. Now
at last for some of them it was to be gratified. The Royal Regiment of
Canada, the Essex Scottish Regiment, the Royal Hamilton Light Infantry, the South Saskatchewan Regiment, the Queen's Own Cameron
Highlanders of Canada, the Fusiliers Mont-Royal, and, since the use of
tanks was part of the plan, the 14th Canadian Army Tank Battalion
(Calgary Regiment) were chosen from the First Canadian Army, from
an Army Tank Brigade, to form by far the larger part of the force to
attack Dieppe. To these were added detachments from many other units
and corps.

Blueprint for a Combined Operation

Once detailed, the troops immediately began an intensive course of
training which, though they did not know it at the time, was in fact a
prolonged rehearsal or rather series of rehearsals for the operation. While
they were thus engaged, the transformation of the Outline Plan into

the Detailed Plan was proceeding under the close direction of the three Force Commanders. These were: for the Navy, Captain J. Hughes Hallett, who was the chief naval planner at Combined Operations Headquarters; for the Army, Major-General J. H. Roberts, M.C., commanding a Division of the First Canadian Army; and for the Air, Air Vice-Marshal (now Air Marshal) T. Leigh Mallory, C.B., D.S.O., then commanding No. 11 Group, Fighter Command, and now Commander-in-Chief, Fighter Command.

The plans were necessarily elaborate. In making them, the Force Commanders and their staffs had the help of intelligence collected by Combined Operations Headquarters. The information supplied was as full and complete as possible. Reports on the nature and size of the landing places were provided, illustrated by photographs and giving details concerning such vital matters as, for example, the tides and tidal streams flowing round the beaches. Maps and plans of the town and its neighbourhood, with the enemy's defences marked upon them, were got ready. Throughout the period of planning, information of all kinds was got together, sifted and passed on, almost daily. Much of it was derived from air photographs, some of them taken from a very low level, 36 hours before the raid. Special models of the coastline were constructed. Nothing which could contribute to the instruction of the attacking troops, from the whereabouts and composition of the heavy coast-defence batteries to the size of the shingle on the beaches, was omitted. Detailed orders covering every phase of the operation were drawn up by the Force Commanders and issued. These took as full account as possible of all the factors calculated and set down by the planners. The most important point was to ensure the correct and accurate timing of each successive phase of the operation. Synchronisation was the keynote. The timings were carefully worked out and had to be adhered to very closely.

While the troops, still in complete ignorance of the real object of their exercises, were engaged in practising climbing up steep places, street fighting, negotiating wire, attacking pillboxes, advancing with tanks, handling weapons of all kinds—they carried out two full-dress rehearsals —and while the staffs were perfecting the plans and drafting the orders for their execution, large quantities of stores ranging from ammunition for the 6-pounder guns in the tanks to the self-heated containers of food to be carried in the landing craft, were being collected in secret.

The assault by the Army was to be made by landing at eight places

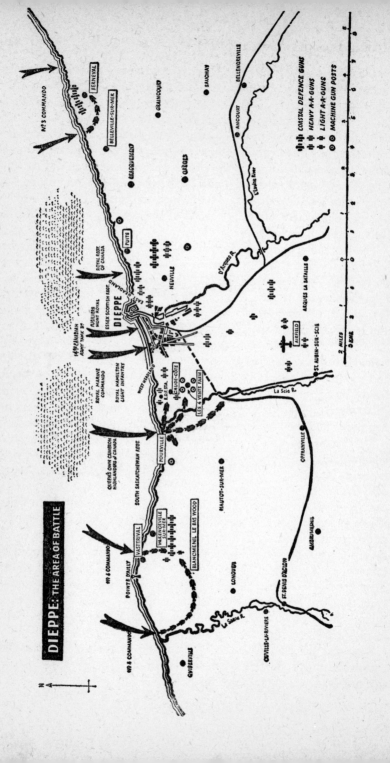

DIEPPE: THE AREA OF BATTLE

N

COASTAL DEFENCE GUNS
HEAVY A-A-GUNS
LIGHT A-A-GUNS
MACHINE GUN POSTS

0   1   2 MILES

N° 3 COMMANDO

BERNEVAL
BELLEVILLE-SUR-MER
BRACQUEMONT
PUITS
ROYAL REGT.
OF CANADA

BELLENGREVILLE
ANCOURT
SAUCHAY
GRAINCOURT
ORGES
NEUVILLE

L'Eaulne River
D'Arques R.
ARQUES LA BATAILLE

FUSILIERS
MONT ROYAL
ESSEX SCOTTISH REGT.
DIEPPE
EAST

14TH CANADIAN
ARMY TANK B⁹

ROYAL MARINE COMMANDO
ROYAL HAMILTON
LIGHT INFANTRY

WEST HEADLAND
L.O.S. STA.
CAUDE-CÔTE
LES 4 VENTS FARM

AIRFIELD
ST. AUBIN-SUR-SCIE
La Scie R.

QUEEN'S OWN CAMERON
HIGHLANDERS of CANADA

SOUTH SASKATCHEWAN REGT.

POURVILLE
HAUTOT-SUR-MER
OFFRANVILLE

N° 4 COMMANDO
VASTERIVAL
POINTE D'AILLY
VARENGEVILLE-SUR-MER
BLANCMENIL LE BAS WOOD

AMBRUMESNIL
ST. DENIS D'ACLON

LONGUEIL
La Saâne R.

N° 3 COMMANDO
QUIBERVILLE
COLMESNIL-LA-RIVIÈRE

on the coast at or near Dieppe. There were to be two outer flank attacks, one at Berneval and Belleville-sur-Mer to the east of the port and the other at Varengeville and a point near the mouth of the River Saane, to the west. These attacks were to be delivered by No. 3 and No. 4 Commandos respectively with the object of destroying the two coast-defence batteries of 5.9 guns, whose fire, as has already been explained, would make it impossible for ships to remain within their range during daylight. In addition to the two outer flank attacks, there were to be two inner attacks delivered at Puits to the east and Pourville to the west of Dieppe. Both these places are small villages, noted in peacetime for their good bathing facilities.

The Royal Regiment of Canada was to land at Puits, seize another heavy coast-defence battery, situated some distance inland, and capture the headland overlooking Dieppe to the east. The South Saskatchewan Regiment was to capture Pourville and a similar headland overlooking Dieppe on the west, destroying on their way a radio-location station and a battery of light anti-aircraft guns. When this regiment had seized the village of Pourville, the Queen's Own Cameron Highlanders of Canada were to pass through them, move down the valley of the Scie and capture the airfield of St. Aubin. The main assault was to be delivered on the town of Dieppe itself, the Essex Scottish Regiment being detailed to land on the eastern half of the long beach which fronts the Esplanade and the Royal Hamilton Light Infantry on the western half.

The landings were to be preceded by a short and intense naval bombardment followed by a concentrated attack of cannon-firing Spitfires and Hurricanes on the main defences behind the beach at Dieppe, delivered at the moment when the landing craft were touching down. A curtain of smoke was to be laid across the eastern headland from which it was expected that the heaviest fire would come. As soon as the two regiments had landed and cleared the beach, the tanks were to be put ashore from the tank landing craft, enter the town and support the infantry in seizing and holding it while the various objectives already mentioned were being blown up. Out at sea, ready in their landing craft, the Fusiliers Mont-Royal were to wait as a floating reserve. Behind them was the Royal Marine Commando, carried in small fast motor boats, manned by the Fighting French.

Such was the plan as finally adopted, and on the night of the 18th-19th August, 1942, the first moment at which the weather was reasonably favourable, it was put into execution.

Throughout the warm summer day of Tuesday the 18th, stores were being loaded, troops going on board. The tanks were already in their landing craft. The force which put to sea as dusk fell that evening was of the most varied kind. Infantry landing ships were filled with armed men and the drab panoply of modern war: at their davits swung the landing craft which would put these men and weapons ashore. More landing craft of other shapes and sizes were spread over the sea nearby, moving forward in ordered lines, and in the rear steamed the blunt-nosed vessels carrying the tanks. All these bore troops, Canadians, Special Service troops, some Fighting French, and a detachment of tough American Rangers.

Escorting the carrying craft were motor gunboats, motor launches, destroyers, seven of the Royal Navy and one of the Polish Navy, a gunboat and a sloop. Of the destroyers, two—H.M.S. "Calpe" and H.M.S. "Fernie"—were respectively the Headquarter ship and the reserve Headquarter ship. On board the former were the Naval and Military Force Commanders and their staffs. On moving to take station as part of the escorting force, "Fernie," being a Hunt class destroyer, played her battle cry on the loud hailer, and as she steamed out of the harbour "the brave sound of the fanfare echoed across the water to the troops embarking at the jetties." By moonrise, well over 200 vessels were moving steadily through the silvered darkness towards the enemy.

15. THE BATTERY DID NOT FIRE AGAIN

In the van were the 9th and 13th mine-sweeping flotillas, which cleared a path through a suspected enemy minefield. Once through it, the Force formed up in a pre-arranged order, the two Commandos who were to make the outer flank landings being to port and starboard of the van. The hours went by, and as the night drew on towards morning it seemed that surprise would be achieved. At 3.47 a.m., however, the group of landing craft belonging to the 1st and 24th Flotillas, some of the crews of which belonged to the Royal Canadian Naval Volunteer Reserve, were suddenly illuminated by star shell. By then they were some seven miles from the coast of France. They had run into a small enemy force of armed trawlers; thus did fortune deal us an evil stroke at a critical moment.

The German ships opened a heavy fire. The landing craft were being led in by a gunboat, on whose bridge Commander D. B. Wyburd, R.N., in charge of the Group, was standing. He pressed on steadily, determined to fight his way through. More German ships joined in the fight until the gunboat was being fiercely attacked by at least five of the enemy. She held on her course for ten minutes, during which time she was their main target and was hit repeatedly, all her guns and wireless equipment being put out of action. Very fortunately, though nearly half were wounded, only one of her company was killed. By seven minutes past four she was a shambles, and was forced to turn away, her speed reduced to six knots. Help was at hand, however. A support craft, one of those to be used to provide covering fire at the moment of landing, engaged the German trawlers, sank one of them and almost certainly another, and damaged others.

By this time, however, the landing craft were scattered. They carried the officers and men of No. 3 Commando whose duty it was to capture the battery near Berneval. It was getting light, and it was now obvious that surprise could not be achieved in this sector. Many of the landing craft had been damaged in this short and sharp encounter. Of these, one carried an officer, a sergeant and 20 other ranks of No. 3 Commando. A shell killed the Army officer and all the crew except the Naval officer in command, who was severely wounded. The sergeant—his name was Collins—took charge: using an Army prismatic compass, for the boat's compass had been damaged, he swung her round, set a course for the port from which he had sailed, and reached it nearly six hours later.

Six landing craft made a landing in broad daylight 25 minutes late on one of the two chosen beaches near Berneval, and a seventh at the other. The six, which through the mischance of the naval action, arrived late, came under heavy fire. They were led in by Lieutenant-Commander C. L. Corke, R.N.V.R., covered by the fire of Motor Launch 346, which subsequently engaged and drove ashore a small armed German tanker, the "Franz." Lieutenant-Commander Corke was soon mortally wounded, his coxswain killed and the wheel taken by a private soldier. The troops were landed from the craft, which was in a sinking condition. Lieutenant-Commander Corke gave orders for the wounded to be transferred to another craft; but he, a dying man, would endanger no man's life, and so he remained where he was alone and went down with his ship.

No. 3 Commando at Berneval

The men who were thus put ashore belonged, for the most part, to No. 6 Troop of No. 3 Commando. Captain R. L. Wills, the Senior Officer present, put himself at their head. The Troop attempted to reach a cleft in the cliff and scale it. It was broad daylight and the enemy were roused and ready. Under withering fire, the Commando advanced and one of them, Corporal Halls, stormed a machine-gun post single-handed. Captain Wills fell, hit in the throat, and Corporal Halls sought to drag him under cover until ordered by his officer, before he lost consciousness, "to get on with the battle." Lieutenant E. D. Loustalot, of the United States Rangers, some 40 of whom were in action for the first time with their British comrades, then took over and displayed much coolness and gallantry, for the first and unhappily the last time. He was shortly afterwards killed. The Commando fought on, unable to make headway against resolute defenders well placed and with every natural and artificial advantage on their side. Eventually those of No. 6 Troop who survived, most of them wounded, surrendered.

Though No. 3 Commando fared so ill on this beach, it had a larger measure of success at the other chosen landing-place, that to which one landing craft had made after the naval encounter. This craft, under the command of Lieutenant H. T. Buckee, R.N.V.R., had on board it Major P. Young, M.C., with two officers and 17 men who formed the Headquarters party of part of the attacking force. Throughout the action at sea, Lieutenant Buckee had maintained a steady course, and had not been seen by the enemy. At ten minutes past four he and those with him found themselves alone. In the shadowy twilight hour before dawn he saw and recognised a gap in the cliffs ahead. There was the beach. He turned to Major Young, pointed to their destination and said that his orders were to put them ashore at all costs. Major Young replied that his orders were to go ashore at all costs. Five minutes before zero hour, the craft touched down, and the party jumped on to the stones.

They had with them ten rifles, a Bren gun, six tommy guns, three pistols and two mortars with only a few bombs. With these, they set out to attack a battery held, as they knew, by some 200 of the enemy. The only way to the top of the cliff was up a steep gully which, when they reached it, was found to be choked with wire. They had with them neither Bangalore torpedoes nor cutters with which to blow it to pieces or hew a path through it, so instead they made use of it. Many of its strands were stretched taut and firmly attached to the sides of the gully. What was designed as a hindrance proved a help, and up this barbed, uncertain rope they climbed. It took them three-quarters of an hour. On reaching the top they went into a wood and thence to the village of Berneval. There they tried to establish the Bren gun on the tower of the village church, but there was no way up to its top, so after exchanging greetings with the local inhabitants, they moved off through orchards into a cornfield. Not 200 yards away was the battery they were to attack, firing at our ships at sea.

That fire soon became very ragged as the Commando soldiers began to snipe the gunners. It was impossible to rush the battery, for the garrison out-numbered them by ten to one, but they were determined to prevent the enemy from shelling the ships at sea. Every time a gun was re-loaded or a man moved, they opened up with their rifles, the Bren and the tommy guns. Under this goad the Germans presently turned one of their guns round, and opened fire at point-blank range on their persistent attackers. It was impossible, however, sufficiently to depress its muzzle and the shells whistled harmlessly over the heads of Major Young and his men, to burst somewhere in France. Nearly two hours passed and ammunition began to run low. It was time to go home;

so back they went, withdrawing in the manner they had so often practised, followed at a respectful distance by some of the enemy. Down
the gully they climbed.

One of them trod on a land-mine which they had missed in the darkness of the ascent, but the wound did not incapacitate him, and setting
up the 3-inch mortar which had been left behind on the beach because
of its weight, he engaged the battery until all his ammunition was
exhausted. At the beach itself Lieutenant Buckee was waiting. He had
lain off for three hours under fire. The Commando soldiers waded out,
and all of them re-embarked. In the words of the official report, "it
[the attack] was not crowned with success, but there is no doubt that
the sniping tactics employed by Major Young and his men greatly inter-
fered with the handling of the battery for upwards of an hour and a half,
during the crucial period of the main landing." Lieutenant Buckee and
Major Young received the Distinguished Service Order.

Double Assault on the West Flank

No. 4 Commando was engaged upon a similar task ten miles away
to the south-west. Here, near Varengeville, was the second coast-defence
battery whose destruction was so necessary. It was of six guns sighted
so as to fire at any ship approaching to within 9,000 yards of Dieppe, and
was defended by wire, pillboxes and two "flak towers" of concrete. Like
the battery at Berneval, it was to be subjected to a double assault. No. 4
Commando, 250 strong, under the command of Lieutenant-Colonel
Lord Lovat, M.C., was to land at two points, one close to the little village
of Vasterival, the other nearly a mile away, about 600 yards from the
mouth of the River Saane.

They were carried towards France in an infantry landing ship, and
at the appointed place and hour they entered their assault craft which
were lowered into the dark sea. "Sitting all orderly" on the hard benches,
like the men of Odysseus on another, if longer, voyage of adventure, they
swept forward in exact formation, led in by an M.G.B. For some time
nothing was to be seen save the wake, faintly phosphorescent, made by
the craft rushing over the dark sea. Some of the men on board presently
fell into a doze, to be awakened by spray breaking over them. Presently
they sighted three darkened ships between them and the shore, and
altered course to starboard to avoid them. At that moment star shell and
tracer lit the sky some miles away to the north-east. The darkened ships
made off to join in the battle thus disclosed and the flotilla, finding its

correct course by means of the lighthouse on the Pointe d'Ailly, which was now visible, approached the beaches. Some on board heard air-raid sirens sounding as they went in, and three Hurricane bombers were seen in the grey light of dawn above the lighthouse, near which was situated the Forward Observation Post of the battery.

As has already been said, the assault was to be made by two parties. What befell those who landed at Vasterival must first be described. Under the command of Major D. Mills-Roberts, they reached land three minutes late and soon discovered that, of the three clefts behind the short beach, the right hand one afforded the best possibilities. True, it was choked with wire, but they had Bangalore torpedoes. Two of these were placed in position and exploded just as cannon fighters from 129 Squadron came in to attack the battery. The noise of this attack mingled with the noise made by the exploding Bangalore torpedoes and thus confused the enemy. Lieutenant D. C. W. Style and his men climbed swiftly up the cleft, closely followed by Major Mills-Roberts with the mortar section under the command of Lieutenant J. F. Ennis. They pushed through a wood until they reached a position so close to the battery that they could hear the words of command given to the German gunners.

At ten minutes to six a brisk small-arms fire was opened on the enemy. The mortars were set up and at the third shot from the two-inch mortar, Troop-Sergeant-Major Dunning with Private Dale and Private Horn dropped a bomb in the middle of the cordite charges and shells stacked alongside the guns ready for use. There was a blinding explosion and the battery did not fire again. The German gunners made every effort to put out the fire thus caused and were sniped, notably by Lance-Corporal Mann, who, with his face and hands painted green, lay up in some bushes a hundred and fifty yards away. His shooting was deadly and equalled only by that of Gunner McDonough, who fired about 60 rounds from an anti-tank rifle against the two flak towers. At 6.20 a.m. a cluster of white Very lights, which was the signal that Lord Lovat was about to launch his attack from the rear of the battery, was seen. The immediate task of Major Mills-Roberts and his men was over. They loosed off a number of smoke bombs and then ceased fire so as not to run the risk of hitting those who were assaulting the battery from the rear.

These attackers formed the larger part of No. 4 Commando, which had landed at the second landing place, not far from the mouth of the

River Saane. After subduing a pillbox near the beach and cutting the telephone and telegraph lines, they pushed on inland for about a mile, following the marshy banks of the river. They then turned left-handed, entered Blancmenil-le-Bas Wood and were now directly behind the German battery. Two of their scouts, pushing forward, came across some 35 Stosstruppen (assault troops), part of the battery's garrison, who were forming up behind a farmhouse with the obvious intention of delivering a counter-attack on Major Mills-Roberts and his galling mortars. The Germans were wiped out where they stood by tommy-gun fire. The Commando—it was composed of "B" and "F" Troops—now formed up in readiness to charge the battery. A number of them, including some American Rangers, were established in some nearby farms, from which they kept up a heavy fire on the enemy.

"We got to a little farm built round a yard," says Corporal Koons, probably the first soldier of the United States Army to kill a German in this war. "We found a small stable into which we put the wounded . . . and there I found a splendid spot for sniping. It was over a manger, and I fired through a slit in the brick wall. I had not been there long when I saw the battery receive a tremendous plastering by bombs from the mortars." A moment later, cannon-firing Spitfires of 129 Squadron swept in to deliver a low-level attack, which they pressed home despite an attempt by a number of Focke-Wulf 190's to prevent them. This attack was timed to perfection, and the moment it was over "B" and "F" Troops went in with the bayonet.

The Charge Was Pressed Home

The charge was made over 250 yards of open ground and was led by Captain R. G. Pettiward and Lieutenant J. A. MacDonald, both of whom fell dead before the battery was reached. A belt of wire was crossed, in places over the bodies of our dead and wounded. The place of the two officers who had fallen was at once taken by Captain Porteous, who had been acting as liaison between the two parties into which the Commando had been divided. He had already been wounded in the hand, but had killed his assailant with his own bayonet. With him in the lead, the charge was pressed home. The whole garrison, with the exception of four men who were taken prisoner, was shot or bayoneted. One of the first to reach the guns was Captain Porteous who fell unconscious beside them, wounded in both thighs. He received the Victoria Cross.

As soon as the guns were captured, "F" Troop demolished them while "B" Troop held the position and dealt with what remained of the German resistance. By ten minutes to seven, all six guns had been blown up and the Commando withdrew towards the beach at Vasterival, carrying their wounded. Their fallen comrades they collected and laid beside the now useless guns which they had helped to capture. Before they left, the Union Jack was run up over the British dead.

The re-embarkation began at half-past seven, the men having to wade out to the boats because of the fast-ebbing tide. Some of them were up to their necks in water. Many of the wounded were ferried in a collapsible boat paddled by a short red-faced Commando soldier, clad solely in a "Mae West" and a woollen cap. The withdrawal was successfully completed and, by nine o'clock, No. 4 Commando was on the way to England. They had lost five officers and 41 other ranks, two officers and nine other ranks being killed. "This hazardous assault," to quote once more the official report, "was carried out strictly according to plan and may well become a model for future operations of this kind."

So much for the outer flank attacks. One had been completely successful; the other had prevented the enemy from making any effective use of a heavy battery for the most crucial period of the operation.

16. THE CANADIANS GO IN

On the inner flanks, landings were to be made at Puits to the east and Pourville to the west. The Royal Regiment of Canada was detailed to land at Puits. Thence they were to move inland, capture another coastal-defence battery of the same strength as that situated at Berneval, and then take in the rear the eastern headland overlooking the beaches at Dieppe on which the main assault was to be delivered.

In the darkness, some precious time was unfortunately lost in forming up the landing craft on the M.G.B., but this error was soon put right. The flotilla, under the leadership of Lieutenant-Commander H. W. Goulding, D.S.O., R.N.R., followed a course which took it past the piers of Dieppe. The enemy evidently mistook it for one of their own convoys, for the harbour lights were turned on.

Day had dawned when the first wave touched down on the beach, which was 300 yards wide and about 250 yards deep; behind it a road leads inland up a small valley to the village of Puits. About 50 yards from the water's edge, a sea-wall, 100 yards long and 12 feet high, divides the beach into two unequal parts. Scarcely were the first elements of the Royal Regiment of Canada ashore when a withering fire was opened by an enemy ready and waiting. Led by their officers, most of whom became casualties in the first few minutes, the men rushed for the shelter of the wall where they were presently joined by others coming in from the second wave which landed shortly afterwards. But the sea-wall afforded no protection; enfilade fire swept it from the left flank and the casualties began swiftly to mount.

Captain G. G. Sinclair and Lieutenants W. G. R. Wedd and W. C. Patterson did their utmost to blow the wire off the top of the wall with Bangalore torpedoes. Lieutenant Wedd rushed a pillbox, threw a gre-nade through its fire slit, which killed all the garrison, and then fell riddled with bullets. A gap was made by Captain Sinclair in the wire near a flight of steps and through it Corporal Ellis passed unscathed, reaching the shelter of a gully. Using bushes as cover, he pressed on and presently reached the top of a hill where he engaged the enemy with rifle fire from a deserted sniper pit. Finding himself alone, he eventually withdrew and got safely back to the beach.

In the meantime, "C" and "D" Companies, with the Commanding Officer of the Battalion, Lieutenant-Colonel D. E. Catto, had landed on the extreme right of the beach to the west of the sea-wall under the cliffs. They were met by heavy fire and immediately began to suffer losses. After considerable delay, for their Bangalore torpedoes had been lost, some of them, led by their Colonel, cut a path through the wire, scaled the cliff and cleared the enemy out of the houses at the top. They were only a small party of six officers and 15 other ranks, some belonging to the Royal Canadian Artillery, including Captain G. A. Browne, the Forward Observation Officer who was to direct the supporting fire from the destroyer H.M.S. "Garth," and they were soon cut off, for the Germans had covered with a machine gun the gap they had made in the wire and no one could pass up or down.

The Royal Regiment Was Pinned Down

Under Lieutenant-Colonel Catto they moved westward along the cliff top, using the cover afforded by some trees and a wall, to try to make contact with the Essex Scottish Regiment which they hoped had by now been able to penetrate into Dieppe. They soon encountered a strong enemy patrol and lay up in a wood near an anti-aircraft battery. They did not surrender until 4.20 in the afternoon.

In the words of Captain Browne, who had sought vainly to indicate targets to the "Garth," "Owing to the heavy and accurate fire of the enemy, the Royal Regiment of Canada was changed in five minutes from an assault battalion on the offensive to something less than two companies on the defensive, pinned down by fire from positions they could not discover. Notwithstanding this situation, the men followed their leaders smartly whenever they could and when, as was mostly the case, it was impossible to move, they lay still under the heavy fire of mortar bombs, watching for orders from their Platoon and Section Commanders."

Throughout the attack two support craft, No. 8 commanded by Sub-Lieutenant F. J. Keep, R.N.V.R., and No. 25 commanded by Sub-Lieutenant Grant, R.N.V.R., gave covering fire until all their guns were silenced. Farther out to sea, the destroyer H.M.S. "Garth" shelled the headland on the right flank, which was also attacked by cannon Hurricanes of No. 32 Squadron.

It was presently apparent that the landing had failed. A succession of efforts was made to withdraw the troops. A number of landing craft went in under very heavy fire. One of them, loaded with men, received a direct hit as she was moving out, and capsized. A number of men clung to the bottom of this craft and were rescued by a daring effort on the part of some light naval craft a few hours later.

While the Royal Regiment of Canada were thus pinned down to the beach in front of Puits, the second inner flank attack to the west of Dieppe was being delivered by the South Saskatchewan Regiment. It was their task to land at the little watering-place of Pourville, capture it and, moving inland, take and hold a defensive position built round Les-Quatre-Vents Farm. They were also to seize the headland on their left flank overlooking Dieppe on the west. They left their infantry landing ships punctually and moved shoreward, "a warm wind laden with the smell of hayfields blowing upon them from the south." A successful landing was made at Pourville five minutes after zero hour and they encountered very little opposition until they were once ashore. "A" Company was to capture the height on the left flank and destroy a battery of A.A. guns and the R.D.F. Station at Caude Côte near it. "C" Company was to seize Pourville and hold the high ground to the west of the village, while "B" and "D" Companies were to cross the River Scie and attack the position at Les-Quatre-Vents Farm.

At Pourville, as at Puits, a sea-wall divides the beaches. "A" Company soon scaled it by the use of ladders and moved off to attack the high ground, after disposing of a couple of pillboxes. They were held up for some time by a patch of swamp but presently got round this and moved forward under cover of a smoke screen, until at about 6 o'clock they were held up more seriously by a road block which they were unable to outflank. In the heavy fighting that ensued, Private Sawden rushed a pillbox single-handed and killed its garrison of six. While "A" Company were thus striving to reach their objectives, "C" Company had reached the village of Pourville, captured La Maison Blanche and taken a number of prisoners. One of their platoons then established itself on the spur already mentioned to the west of the village.

"B" and "D" Companies went through Pourville until they reached the bridge over the River Scie. Here they were held up by heavy mortar and machine-gun fire, but some crossed the bridge and others swam the river or got over it on rafts. The conduct of the Commanding Officer, Lieutenant-Colonel C. C. I. Merritt, was an example and inspiration to them all. The bridge across the river was a most unhealthy spot. It was under intermittent but often heavy fire. This did not deter Lieutenant-Colonel Merritt. "See," he exclaimed, "there is no danger here," and taking off his steel helmet, he walked over the bridge swinging it in his hand and subsequently crossed and re-crossed four times. "B" and "D" Companies pressed on, fighting with great tenacity. They delivered a number of attacks on the pillboxes covering Les-Quatre-Vents Farm. Some of these were organised by Lieutenant-Colonel Merritt and one was led by Major McTavish. The pillboxes were eventually captured, largely owing to the action of Private Fenner who walked straight for the enemy's position firing a Bren gun from the hip.

Progress, however, had been slow and enemy resistance heavy. The morning passed and by the time the signal to withdraw was received, the farm itself was uncaptured and its garrison still active. Throughout the seven hours during which they were heavily engaged, the South Saskatchewan Regiment accounted for very many of the enemy. They found the German mortar fire exceedingly accurate and well maintained. Their snipers, too, were a nuisance. They were well-trained and resolute men, bold enough to lie quiet until the Canadians had passed them and then swing round to open fire on them from the rear.

Some forty minutes after the South Saskatchewan Regiment had got ashore and seized the bridgehead, a second flight of assault craft carrying the Queen's Own Cameron Highlanders of Canada arrived. It was broad daylight, and as they swept in a piper began to play "The Hundred Pipers" and continued to do so during the landing. They were not met with any great volume of fire but suffered a grievous misfortune at the very outset, for their Commanding Officer, Lieutenant-Colonel A. C. Gostling, was killed as he jumped on to the beach. Under their second-in-command, Major A. T. Law, the Regiment moved briskly forward into Pourville, and a Company soon reinforced the South Saskatchewan Regiment on the east. The remainder of the Battalion pushed on down the valley of the River Scie; but since Les-Quatre-Vents Farm had not been captured, they kept to the west side of the river to avoid, if they could, the volume of fire directed against them from that well-defended enemy position. They pushed on through woods, their objective being the airfield at St. Aubin, some three and a half miles from Pourville.

By 8.45 they had advanced a good part of that distance and were engaged in forcing the passage of the river.

Embarkation Under Heavy Fire

It was, by this time, realised that everything had not gone according to plan, for the tanks which they should have met somewhere in that neighbourhood were nowhere to be seen. They continued, however, to press the attack with great vigour and to inflict heavy casualties on the enemy, until the time for withdrawal, when they started back, suffering losses as they went. These were heavy in "C" Company, which formed the rear guard. When they reached Pourville, they found the all-important western height had been lost. A counter-attack by a battalion of German infantry had driven from it its defenders, "C" Company of the South Saskatchewan Regiment. Thus the enemy were able to dominate, not only the village of Pourville itself, but also the beach from which the withdrawal would have to take place and the slopes to the eastward down which must come "A" and "D" Companies of the South Saskatchewan Regiment.

The casualties were carried down and placed under the cover of the sea-wall, their movement being directed by Lieutenant-Commander R. N. Prior, D.S.O., R.N., and the Assistant Beachmaster, Lieutenant R. D. Millar, R.N.V.R., both of whom showed utter disregard for their own safety and both of whom were wounded. At 10.45, landing craft came in to the beach to take off the troops. They were met with heavy mortar fire, and one was hit and capsized. Others, however, took men on board and cleared the beach successfully, and later a second wave of landing craft appeared. To reach them, the Canadians had to cross 200 yards of open ground and then wade or swim through 150 yards of water, for the state of the tide made it impossible for the craft to come farther in to the shore without the risk of being stranded. Heavy losses were incurred over that open stretch of sand and water. The work of the stretcher bearers at this time was very gallant, as was the conduct of Captain W. A. Hayter, the Medical Officer of the South Saskatche-wans, who had established three Regimental Aid Posts. He moved from one to another of these as opportunity afforded or necessity directed, until he too became a casualty.

About half-past eleven, Lieutenant-Colonel Merritt and Major Orme collected some men and attacked some machine guns to the west of the beach, silencing their fire. By noon, most of the troops had been re-

Zero feet, near zero hour. *Low-flying aircraft took this reconnaissance photograph of Dieppe, 36 hours before the operation began. A German sentry is at the bridgehead.*

The Americans lend a hand. *A bombing attack by U.S. Flying Fortresses knocked out the key airfield at Abbeville for a vital two hours. Bombs can be seen bursting (1) on the north dispersal area, (2) on a runway, (3) on or near enemy flak positions.*

Rendezvous for assault. *A mass of light craft assembled for the attack.*

Into battle. *Under cover of a smoke screen, landing craft leap towards the shore.*

H.Q. LT.COL. LORD L

'B' TROOP

BLANCMENIL
LE BAS WOOD

'F' TROOP

M.G.

BATTERY

MORTAR O.P.
FORCE BATTLE
H.Q.

SECTN
'A' TP

'C' TROOP

'C' TROOP

O.P

VARENGEVILLE

VASTERIVAL

POINTE D'AILL

MAJ. MILLS ROBERTS
SECTION OF 'A' TROOP
AND 'C' TROOP

| 500 | YARDS 0 | 500 | 1000 | 1500 |
| 500 | METRES 0 | 500 | 1000 | |

MAIN ASSAULT

Ste MARGUERITE

R. SAANE

EAST END OF CLIFFS

LT. COL. LORD LOVAT
1 SECTⁿ OF 'A' TROOP
'B' TROOP, 'F' TROOP
H.Q.

	A.A. GUNS		TELEPHONE WIRE
	HEAVY GUNS		XXXXXXX BARBED WIRE
	STRONG POINTS		

2000 2500 3000 3500 4000
2000 2500 3000 3500

ictly according to plan." *The double assault by No. 4 Commando on the six-gun ery west of Dieppe.*

The Canadians go in. *Quiet, relaxed, seeming almost nonchalant, Canadian troops approach the cliffs of Dieppe.*

Vast ramparts of water, *thrown up by enemy bombing, tower above our attacking craft.*

Withdrawal under fire. *No. 4 Commando re-embarking from Vasterival beach under German fire from the cliff tops. Black smoke from German mortar shells can be seen to the right of the gully down which the troops are withdrawing.*

Journey Home. *L.C.A.s carrying No. 4 Commando, on their way home through the German minefields, save an American airman whose Spitfire has been shot down. An identification strip and smoke canisters can be seen on the stern of the nearest L.C.A. Both pictures are by Sapper Mullen, who was present.*

The Commandos were there. *Officers and men of No. 4 Commando back in Britain after their "model operation" against the battery at Varengeville.*

embarked and only a few remained. These were formed into a rear guard and held a perimeter under the command of Lieutenant-Colonel Merritt aided by Lieutenant-Commander Prior. They held it until their ammunition was exhausted and they were forced to surrender about three o'clock, but their action had enabled many men to be taken off who would have otherwise remained behind. Lieutenant-Colonel Merritt was awarded the Victoria Cross.

Throughout the assault and the evacuation, covering fire had been provided at frequent intervals by the Royal Navy, and many attacks were made by our air squadrons. The fire of H.M.S. "Brocklesby" was effective during the withdrawal, and her guns silenced some of the numerous machine guns and mortars by then in action.

"We Steamed Along as Bold as Brass"

The scene at sea throughout this attack was in striking contrast with that on land. "By now it was broad daylight," says Lieutenant Peter Scott, commanding a gunboat, "and at 0550 a new battery to the east of the lighthouse opened up, and we had to draw yet farther off. All this time there were explosions ashore from mortars, guns and bombs. At times there were great sheets of flame, at others very heavy detonations. All the while, Bostons and Hurribombers kept coming in to attack the defences. One very loud bang was Lord Lovat's Commando blowing up the ammunition dump of the battery he had been detailed to destroy.

"At about six o'clock we sighted another gunboat coming towards us through the smoke to the eastward. This smoke drifted seaward like white mist on the light off-shore breeze. Low-flying aircraft which passed near us turned out to be first Blenheims and later Mustangs. We steamed slowly along the enemy coast as bold as brass. At this moment in the bright morning sunshine we were lulled into a most curious and entirely false sense of security. There, four miles away on our port beam, shone the cliffs and the brilliant summer green of the fields and woods. St. Valéry-en-Caux nestled in its hollow with a haze of chimney smoke above it. We remembered that we had been told that the Luftwaffe would be fully occupied elsewhere, and indeed we had seen the milling clouds of Spitfires arriving as we left. They had come wave upon wave in numbers the like of which I had never before seen. We forgot our own assessment that unprotected ships outside the fighter umbrella would be exactly what the Germans would be looking for.

"We did not imagine, as we might have done, the watchers on the cliff tops feverishly telephoning for the German Air Force to come quickly and bomb the two unprotected ships to the westward. 'Better send someone to get some breakfast for the ship's company, No. 1,' I said, and went on examining the coastline with glasses. A light westerly breeze turned the sea deep purplish-blue. Twelve Bostons flying in perfect formation passed inland high above us, shining in the early sunlight.

"Two aircraft slipped between us and the other gunboat, unseen until they were past, low over the sea. 'Friendly,' said Nigel (my No. 1); but I got the glasses on them and saw the black cross on the side of one —probably F.W. 190's. We altered course off shore for we were not in a healthy place and we suddenly realised it. Two more square-wing-tipped planes came back from the westward—the Mustangs. But a few minutes later there were 'Aircraft right astern.' Two fighters were weaving about and working their way up into the sun. In a few moments it was evident that they had designs upon us, and as they turned their noses down I could see the bomb hanging under the first one. 'Hard a-starboard,' and I increased speed. Off came the bomb just as the guns opened up. It fell in our wake close astern.

The Second Focke-Wulf Attacks

"The second Hun was circling towards the other boat. Whether he misjudged the attack or saw that his mate had missed will never be known, but he transferred his attention to us, coming in on the port bow whilst we still turned to starboard. As he steadied up towards us in a shallow dive I saw splashes in the water short of us, and then our own guns opened up. The F.W.190 was only firing machine gun—not cannon—and he was himself enveloped in a haze of tracer. I saw his bomb take the water 20 yards short on our port beam. There was a pause, and then a heavy shock and a huge waterspout—but the ship was still afloat and still steaming. I remember thinking it must have been a very small bomb not to have damaged us more. Then I looked at the F.W. A trail of wispy black smoke was coming out of it, and it was losing height. But when it was nearly down to the water it picked up again and began to climb. I stopped watching it and became concerned with the fact that the ship would not steer, and that the alarm bells were ringing continuously, that in fact we had been badly shaken. Those in the other gunboat, however, watched the damaged F.W. falter again and crash head-on into the bottom of the cliffs.

"Meanwhile the Chief Engineer had arrived on the bridge. 'I'd like to stop,' he said, 'but we *can* keep going slowly if we must.' I rang down, 'Stop both,' and told the other boat to take us in tow. She came alongside with a rush and a bit of a bump, but five minutes later (and only 14 minutes after the bombing) we were under way in tow—very quick work.

"A quarter of an hour passed. Then Jimmy Grout, Flotilla Engineer Officer, appeared grinning and sweating on the bridge: 'We've found it—you can go ahead in a minute or two,' and he disappeared again like a rabbit. Never was such a report more welcome, for our position was very sticky. We were still in full view of the coast—one F.W. had returned to base to report that we were disabled. It obviously could not be long before further aircraft were sent to complete the job and dispatch us for good. We were still a long way from the fighter umbrella. But ten minutes later the tow had been slipped, and we set off at high speed to the eastward. We were soon closing the escort destroyers and small craft to the N.W. of Dieppe, whilst hordes of Spitfires milled comfortingly overhead. We breathed again."

17. THE BATTLE OF THE SEA–WALL

It is time to turn to the assault on Dieppe itself. This was to be delivered by the Essex Scottish Regiment and the Royal Hamilton Light Infantry. They were to be put ashore on the sea front, where the beach stretches from the west breakwater for 1,700 yards. It ends by the cliffs in the shadow of which stand the Vieux Château and, nearer the sea, the modern Casino. Beyond the beach, and divided from it by a sea-wall, lies the Boulevard Maréchal Foch, bounding one side of the ornamental gardens which stretch inland to the Boulevard de Verdun. This boulevard is backed by houses and hotels, and these the Germans had fortified. It was the task of the two Regiments to seize the beaches, thus enabling the tanks to land, and then to push on and hold the town while the demolitions were being carried out.

They went in together, the Essex Scottish to the left and the Royal Hamilton Light Infantry to the right. The landing was covered by a short, intense bombardment from the destroyers at sea; and as their fire ceased some sixty cannon-firing Spitfires and Hurricanes shot up the houses along the front. While they did so, the eastern headland above Dieppe Harbour was smothered in smoke dropped by three squadrons of Bostons and Blenheims. Immediate fire support was provided by the special craft which went in very close. They carried out this dangerous duty under the point-blank fire of the enemy, which they returned with vigour and considerable effect. All were hit, and one was completely disabled, her Captain, Lieutenant E. L. Graham, R.N.V.R., killed, and her guns put out of action one by one until she finally sank. On the death of her Captain, the only surviving officer, Surgeon-Lieutenant M. P. Martin, took command, remaining on board until the ship went down. He was rescued, reached the "Calpe" and, though himself wounded, continued to help the other surgeons on board until the ship returned to port. He was awarded the Distinguished Service Order.

On reaching the beaches, the Essex Scottish Regiment and the Royal

Hamilton Light Infantry rushed forward, but, as with the Royal Regiment at Puits, they came at once under fierce frontal and enfilade fire. The defences in the houses behind the promenade had been subdued but not silenced by the naval and air bombardment, and the guns were still in action. Moreover, to the eastward, many guns, some of quite considerable calibre, had been mounted in the caves which honeycomb the face of the headland. As the smoke screen drifted away they opened fire with great effect.

The Essex Scottish, being the nearer, suffered the more heavily and could not get farther than the sea-wall dividing the promenade from the beach. Here they were held up by wire, though a small party subsequently penetrated into the town. To their right, some of the Royal Hamilton Light Infantry, led by Captain A. C. Hill and others, stormed the Casino. They were presently joined by a party of Royal Canadian Engineers, led by Sergeant G. A. Hickson. Pillboxes nearby were blown up by the Bangalore torpedoes of the infantry, and Sergeant Hickson's demolition charges quelled all resistance in the Casino itself and destroyed, among other defences, a 4-inch gun. Captain Hill then pressed on into the town with a small party of men, followed by Sergeant Hickson with another party; while a third went forward under Lieutenant L. C. Bell. They eventually reached the Church of St. Rémy, but, being unsupported, could go no further.

Meanwhile, the first wave of tanks had arrived at the beach. They came carried in six tank-landing craft in which, also, were sappers and beach parties. The sappers were to demolish the tank obstacles so that the tanks might pass through the narrow streets of Dieppe. The landing craft were at once heavily fired on, for the defences had not been mastered. They were all hit; one sank, and one remained aground on fire. Nevertheless, all but two of the tanks were successfully landed. The gallantry shown by the crews of the landing craft was of a high order. One of them did not succeed in beaching until the fourth attempt, losing three helmsmen in trying to do so.

The second flight, which landed half an hour later, came under even heavier fire. One landing craft was sunk just off the beach, another made two attempts to put her tanks ashore. On board her, among others, was Brigadier S. Lett, one of the two Brigade Commanders. What happened is best described in the words of Sergeant Badlan of the Royal Marines, who took charge of her when all her crew were killed or wounded—a deed which won him the Distinguished Conduct Medal.

He was part of the Beach Provost Party under the command of Lieu-tenant-Colonel R. G. Parks-Smith, R.M., who was mortally wounded, one of the five officers from the staff of Combined Operations Head-quarters who became casualties during the raid.

After describing how the tank landing craft had put one tank ashore and then made out to sea again, the Sergeant continues: "We received a signal from one unit to say they had captured the Casino on the right and were held up by machine-gun posts, and were asking for assistance. The Brigadier then decided that he would go in and try to land the other two tanks to wipe out the machine-gun posts. We went in alone . . . and steered closer in to the cliffs, perhaps 100 yards to the right of the position we had reached before. We were under heavy fire and there seemed to be a bigger concentration of guns—we were really catching it that time. Before we were 50 yards from the shore we were hit about 20 times. We had quite a lot of holes, and a number of casualties on the port side . . . I was the only one uninjured. We were constantly hit, at least once every minute. . . . We seemed to be going astern to port and the engines were still working, and I thought we should be able to get clear of the beach, so I immediately went to the bridge where I found a Lieutenant-Colonel of the Canadians and an able-seaman, both dead.

"I could not find the wheel on the bridge so I went below . . . there was a small fire burning in the corner, caused by shell splinters. The compass had gone and three port-holes were broken. Different packages belonging to the officers had burst open, and clothes and paper were burning; it was a small fire, and only took two steel helmets full of water to put out. I put the wheel to starboard." (The engines had been reversed by Major M. E. P. Garneau, who had entered the engine room, and being unacquainted with the machinery, altered the posi-tion of every lever he could see until the craft went astern.) "Drawing away from the beach, I saw one of the men in the water catch hold of a rope, and when he got back he turned out to be one of the engine-room mechanics, and he went down to the engine room. I rang full speed ahead and we made our way out again. I did not know which way I was going, as I had no compass, and asked for verbal orders. Sergeant Slade was on the port side and a Canadian officer on the starboard side, trying to tell me how to keep in the centre and out of range of the guns. We went out from the shore zig-zagging. We man-aged to get clear of the coast, and a Naval Sub-Lieutenant, the second-

in-command, returned to the bridge. He had been forward ready to
lower the flap door and had been wounded in the left arm and had a
nasty knock in the right eye. I acted as helmsman while he handled the
ship. . . ."

Tanks Smash into the Town

Altogether, 28 tanks were landed. They were under the command of
Lieutenant-Colonel J. G. Andrews. His tank was about to go ashore
when the ramp chains of the landing craft were cut by gunfire, and
the ramp fell prematurely just as the tank was going through the door.
It fell into eight feet of water and sank. "I am baling out," said Lieutenant-Colonel Andrews over the wireless. He did so with the rest of
his crew, and boarded a motor launch which was at that moment hit and
set on fire. His Commanding Officer's pennant on the wireless mast
remained flying on the submerged tank throughout the day. Several of
the tanks remained on the beach, their tracks having been damaged by
hits. Out of one of them an officer was seen to climb, and, though badly
wounded in the face, climb into the tank immediately behind. Its turret
turned, its six-pounder gun spoke, and the anti-tank gun which had
knocked out the first tank was silenced.

A number got over the sea-wall and found themselves on the esplanade. Some turned west and attacked the defences on the western
headland, others made for the town itself. The casualties among the
Sappers, however, had been so heavy that none was available to destroy
the tank blocks at the end of the narrow streets leading from the Boulevard de Verdun, and the stretch of garden in front of it, into the town.
One tank, however, commanded by Lieutenant A. B. Patterson, smashed
through a house and got into the town, followed probably by two
more. Other tanks moved up and down the esplanade firing at the
German defences until their ammunition was exhausted. Though the
tanks did considerable execution, and silenced the defences in places,
they were unable to give adequate support since the anti-tank defences
had not been overcome. Behind the road blocks on the Boulevard de
Verdun were anti-tank guns, and more of these weapons were hidden
in the caves of the eastern headland, whence their fire was the more
deadly because they could not be accurately located and engaged.

By half-past six in the morning, the Force Commanders on H.M.S.
"Calpe" were well aware that the situation was not developing as well
as had been hoped. No word had come from the Royal Regiment at

Puits or from No. 3 Commando at Berneval. On the other hand, the situation at Pourville, where the South Saskatchewan Regiment and the Queen's Own Cameron Highlanders of Canada were engaged, appeared not unfavourable. It was known, too, that No. 4 Commando had landed successfully at Vasterival. The Military Force Commander decided that the time had come to make use of his reserves. They consisted, in the first place, of the Fusiliers Mont-Royal, a famous French-Canadian Regiment. At that moment, the fire on the eastern half of the main beach in front of Dieppe had slackened somewhat. It seemed to Major-General Roberts that if the Essex Scottish could be reinforced, they would be able to capture the vital eastern headland, especially now that they had tanks to help them, for he had just received a message to say that they were ashore.

Reserves Are Sent In

The Fusiliers Mont-Royal were accordingly sent in and landed soon after seven o'clock, losing two landing craft on the way. The fire on the beaches, however, as soon as they set foot on them, proved to be as fierce as ever. Some found cover behind stranded tanks, others in folds of the shingle. Their Commanding Officer, Lieutenant-Colonel D. Menard, was wounded. A strong westerly set of the tide had taken more than half of them to the west of the Casino where they eventually got ashore, not on the main beach but on a small stretch of shingle and rock beneath high, unscalable cliffs. There they were cut off, for they had no room to deploy, and whenever they sought to move to a flank, they were met with heavy machine-gun and mortar fire directed upon them from positions at the top of the cliff, which they could not see and therefore could not engage. They eventually surrendered about noon, after more than a hundred had been wounded.

Two other parties of the Fusiliers Mont-Royal, one commanded by Captain G. Vandelac and the other by Sergeant Dubuc, had better fortune. They had landed almost opposite the Casino which, by the time they reached it, was in our hands. They pushed on, therefore, Captain Vandelac to attack some of the houses on the Boulevard de Verdun, and Sergeant Dubuc to penetrate much farther into the town. With eleven men, he turned east and reached the Bassin du Canada, part of Dieppe's inner harbour. The party had had to fight its way step by step, and in doing so destroyed a German machine-gun post at a street corner. Arrived at the edge of the dock basin, the Fusiliers killed or wounded all the Germans seen on the barges and small craft lying there. They then pressed on until they encountered superior German forces. By then, they had no more ammunition and were forced to surrender.

The Germans made them take off their clothes. When stripped to their underwear, they were lined up facing a wall and left in charge of a single German soldier. When the other Germans had left, Sergeant Dubuc distracted the sentry's attention. As soon as he had turned his head, the Fusiliers fell upon him as one man, killed him and made off in their pants and vests through the town for the beach. Several lost themselves, but Sergeant Dubuc reached the margin of the sea where he found his Commanding Officer grievously wounded. It was now after eleven o'clock, and the evacuation had begun. Disobeying Lieutenant-Colonel Menard's order to leave him where he was, Sergeant Dubuc got him safely on to an assault landing craft and himself went on board another, carrying a badly wounded Corporal. In this fashion, he returned to England and was subsequently awarded the Military Medal.

Despite the efforts of the Fusiliers Mont-Royal, the eastern headland still remained untaken, and soon after seven o'clock, Major-General Roberts decided to reinforce again, this time with the Royal Marine Commando. By then he knew that No. 4 Commando had destroyed the heavy battery at Varengeville, that the Camerons were through Pourville which was in the hands of the South Saskatchewan Regiment, that the Casino in front of Dieppe itself was captured, and that the Tobacco Factory together with other buildings in the centre of the German defences behind the promenade was on fire.

The Battle Spluttered and Rumbled

Like everyone else on board the ships, he could see but little. Dieppe was shrouded in smoke behind which the battle spluttered and rumbled. It seemed to the Military Force Commander that, now the Casino was captured and the tanks were over the esplanade, there was still a good chance that he might seize the town. At that time, he did not know that the Essex Scottish and the Fusiliers Mont-Royal had been unable to subdue the eastern headland, but he knew that it was being attacked. There was a reasonable prospect, or so it appeared, that the Royal Hamilton Light Infantry, if reinforced, would be able to capture the western headland. The Royal Marine Commando was accordingly sent in to help them to do so.

They were collected from the Fighting French *chasseurs,* in which they had been taken to Dieppe, and trans-shipped into landing craft detailed from the Boat Pool. This Pool had been established, in accordance with the plan, as soon as the landings had taken place. The small craft lay in it, protected from the fire of the enemy by continuous smoke screens laid at frequent intervals by the destroyers. It took some time to collect the craft and it was not until about half past eight that the Royal Marine Commando was ready to move in to land.

"By that time," says Lieutenant Scott, "the westerly wind was now falling light as the sun blazed hotter. The sea was glass calm. Cloud upon cloud of Spitfires circled above between three and ten thousand feet. There were no enemy aircraft in sight at all. The Hun flak was still lively whenever our fighters or fighter bombers went low over Dieppe—especially to the eastward. Every 20 minutes or so a fresh bunch of Hurricane bombers came in low from the sea and shot up and bombed the defences ashore. I saw one of these hit and watched him circle very slowly before crashing into the trees.

"Presently a Dornier came very low along the coast. It was spotted by some Spitfires, one of which was soon on its tail. Smoke came first from the Spitfire—probably smoke from his own cannon—and then from the Dornier, which at once caught fire and went straight down into the wood behind the Phare D'Ailly. A huge cloud of dark-brown smoke burst into the sky and curled up from the burning wreck. We 'closed' the 'Calpe,' struggling with our loud-hailing equipment which remained resolutely silent. She was lying stopped and was surrounded by assault landing craft, R boats, M.L.s and M.G.B.s, tank and support landing craft. Some were alongside, others lay round the other destroyers, two or three of which were in sight.

"A smoke screen began inshore of the assembled pool of craft and drifted sluggishly north-east; but to the south and south-west the coast, no more than a mile away, was clearly visible in every detail. No sign of opposition there; Lord Lovat's party had done their job.

"The feeling of peaceful activity was most strange and incongruous. The smoke itself was white and friendly—the protecting aircraft circled unmolested, and the boat pool of perhaps 50 or 60 craft was equally unmolested. The sun was so hot and the sea so smooth that 'Hands to bathe' would have seemed a perfectly appropriate signal. We leaned lazily on the bridge screen waiting for orders from the 'Calpe,' whilst even the din of the battle to the eastward seemed to be muffled by the smoke. The boat pool had drifted to the westward so that it lay between Pourville and the D'Ailly Lighthouse. How inviting looked the luxurious woods on top of the cliff and the brilliant fields, but the powers that be wanted them blotted out. 'Maintain a smoke screen half a mile inshore and to the westward,' came over the loud hailer from the 'Calpe.' "

"A Courage Terrible to See"

From this scene of seeming summer peace, the Royal Marine Commando moved forward in their landing craft through the smoke. At first it afforded them cover, and fire support was given to them by the river gunboat "Locust," two support craft and the Fighting French *chasseurs*; but when they cleared the last of the smoke screens, enemy guns of all descriptions, from light A.A. to rifles, opened a murderous fire. This was returned with Bren guns from the deck of the landing craft. Marines Breen and Bradshaw particularly distinguished themselves by the manner in which they kept their guns in action from positions utterly devoid of cover. To quote, again, the official report: " 'With a courage terrible to see,' the Marines went in to land determined, if fortune so willed, to repeat at Dieppe what their fathers had accomplished at Zeebrugge." But fortune was against them. Few who reached the beach survived unhurt. Of those who did, Lieutenant K. W. R. Smale, R.M., with two non-commissioned officers and the remains of his platoon, engaged the enemy with Bren guns from behind a stranded L.C.T.

Not all the landing craft had reached the shore. Many were still coming in with great resolution under this heavy fire. On board one of them was the Officer Commanding, Lieutenant-Colonel J. P. Phillips. In the sunlight striking the beaches and houses of Dieppe with all the greater brilliance after the darkness of the smoke through which he had just passed, he saw the true gravity of the situation. Far from being clear of the enemy, the beach was swept by their concentrated fire. Realising that the situation was not what the Military Force Commander had visualised, he determined to halt the landing if he could. By then his craft was close in shore. Putting on a pair of white gloves so that his hands could be the more easily seen, he jumped on to the forward deck and signalled to the remaining craft to put about and return to the smoke screen. They saw his hands moving and understood his meaning. As they began to turn, he fell mortally wounded. By his action, he had

saved some two hundred of his men from entering a fire which must
have proved mortal to very many of them.

By now it was obvious that the headlands to the east and west of
Dieppe would not be captured in time to permit an entry into the town;
the doors were, in fact, still closed. It was decided to withdraw those
who had been assaulting them and the town so intrepidly.

18. THE TRIUMPH IN THE AIR

It must be borne in mind that all this time an air battle of gradually increasing intensity had been going on overhead since the first glimmer of dawn. It began somewhat slowly, if that term can be applied to a fight in the air. The enemy were not prepared, and at the beginning brought no more than 25 to 30 fighters on the scene. These presently increased to between 50 and 100, including fighter-bombers; but it was not until ten o'clock in the morning that the first German bombers appeared. By that time, our aircraft had been flying in great strength over a part of the enemy's occupied territory for five hours. They were to continue to do so until nightfall. In addition to the bombing of the different batteries, the shooting-up of the houses behind the promenade of Dieppe and the laying of smoke over the eastern headland, tasks which have already been described, a constant and very efficient air umbrella was being maintained above our Naval Forces. No enemy aircraft was allowed near them if it could be driven off, and not many got through.

Though damage was caused by near misses to several craft, the only major success which the German Air Force can claim is the sinking of the "Berkeley," and that in itself was an accident. Soon after one o'clock in the forenoon she was hit and badly damaged by a bomb from a Junkers 88, which had jettisoned its load on being attacked by one of our Spitfires. By ill luck, the "Berkeley" happened to be underneath when the bombs fell. Her bridge was destroyed. Among others, Wing-Commander S. H. Skinner was killed and Lieutenant-Colonel L. B. Hillsinger of the U.S. Army Air Corps wounded. They were both from the staff of Combined Operations Headquarters. Lieutenant-Colonel Hillsinger was wearing a pair of smart new shoes. When he came to, after the explosion of the bomb, he saw his left foot floating past with one of them on it. This enraged him, and he took off his other shoe and flung it after his foot in disgust. He was taken aboard an M.G.B., and refusing to go below, lay on deck directing the A.A. fire of the ship.

He was awarded the U.S. Distinguished Service Cross and the Order of the Purple Heart.

A Battle of Britain in Reverse

At 10.30 the American Army Air Force lent a hand. Twenty-four Fortresses, escorted by four squadrons of Spitfires, bombed the nearest enemy airfield at Abbeville-Drucat with such good effect that 16 aircraft, at least, were destroyed or damaged at the dispersal points, and the airfield itself put out of action for a vital two hours. More than that, the controllers of the whole of that fighter area appear to have been killed or wounded, for the control remained out of action until the evening, when a new and unfamiliar voice came on the air.

Throughout the action up to the hour of withdrawal, the Air Force received frequent requests for curtains of smoke to be laid, mainly on the eastern headland, and for batteries to be bombed. These requests were met to the limit. Many had been anticipated, for Air Vice-Marshal Leigh Mallory, in his Headquarters at No. 11 Group, could see with great clarity every move of the battle as it took place before him on the great map. Throughout the operation, he knew exactly what was happening and was able to anticipate every move of the enemy in the air. He was, in fact, fighting one day of the "Battle of Britain," only the other way round. His forces were the attackers, the Germans were on the defensive. Altogether his aircraft made over 2,000 sorties. Among them, special mention must be made of the reconnaissance aircraft of Army Co-operation Command, two squadrons of which came from the R.C.A.F. These American-built Mustangs ranged far and wide over Northern France. It was among them that the heaviest casualties were sustained, for they were flying alone, outside and far beyond the main area of air cover.

Between dawn and dusk our aircraft accounted for 93 German aircraft known to be destroyed—43 of them bombers, a further 44 probably destroyed, and 148 damaged. There is evidence to show that the German loss in aircraft destroyed may have been as high as 170. Our own aircraft losses were 98.

The Withdrawal Was a Tough Business

To return to the withdrawal. That of Nos. 3 and 4 Commandos and of the two Canadian battalions at Pourville has already been described. The withdrawal from the main beaches was timed to begin at 11 a.m., when a curtain of smoke was laid between the headlands by Bostons of 411 Squadron. It was carried out with great difficulty in the face of the heaviest fire from an enemy unsubdued and still vigorous. The Royal Hamilton Light Infantry moved back to the sea-shore from the Casino under the leadership of Captain J. M. Currie and Major H. F. Lazier. Detachments of this Regiment and of the Fusiliers Mont-Royal held the Casino until the last. Among the last to leave was Sergeant-Major Dumais, of the Fusiliers Mont-Royal, who withdrew his men to the beach and got them on board a landing craft, but was unable by reason of the weight of his equipment to pull himself on deck, and remained behind. He was taken prisoner.

Sentences, taken at random from the reports of men who returned from the beaches, indicate the conditions under which the withdrawal had to take place.

". . . I made my way out to an L.C.A., but the first one I came to was hit and I was knocked off it. I was picked up by another which was over-crowded and sinking, but another craft came alongside and took off most of the men, leaving the rest of us to bale out until we attracted the attention of a further ship, which stopped and took us on board. . . ."

"We got back to the beach and out to an L.C.A. Before I got in, it pulled out and I hung on to some ropes and was pulled in. A bullet hit me in the arm and knocked me off the rope, but I managed to grab the iron bars by the propeller, and after it had pulled me a long way a couple of people pulled me up over the back, and that L.C.A. brought me to Newhaven. . . ."

"Nous sommes rembarqués sous un feu intense de la mitraille et de mortier . . . je suis embarqué sur un L.C.A. que j'ai quitté dix minutes après parce qu'il coulait. . . ."

"As soon as the L.C.A. arrived we went through smoke and helped as many wounded as we could to the boats. On the boats heavy fire continued and casualties were quite heavy."

By twenty minutes past twelve most of the men who had fought their way back to the main beaches had been got away by the crews of the landing craft, "who," says the official report, "showed complete disregard of danger in their efforts to take off the troops."

Throughout the day and especially during the period of re-embarkation the work of the medical officers and orderlies with the Royal Canadian Army Medical Corps was of the highest order. The number of wounded was high, medical supplies ran short on the beach, and large dressings were much in demand. Captain D. W. Clare with Honorary Captain J. W. Foote, Chaplain of the Royal Hamilton Light Infantry, and Corporal A. W. Comfort, who did not belie his name, aided the wounded. Many of them owe their lives to these men.

Shortly before one o'clock, the Naval Force Commander decided to make one further effort to take more men off. "Now Dieppe is shrouded in a pall of smoke, fog and haze," says the log of Lieutenant R. H. M. Boyle, R.N.V.R., who was serving on board the "Calpe," "even in the bit of land you could see there are things smoking everywhere. We hope to go in again and fetch more men off still there. . . . Receive terrific fire from beach, but we fire back with forrard guns. (Rather difficult to write!)

1258. Attack by bombers as usual, we return a good fire and get some hits.
1301. Another Dornier over. All bombs miss and he is hit.
1302. We send out a thick smoke screen. All the time A.A. shells are bursting over us.
1315. Three more Dorniers with bombs, all miss, no planes hit either.
1320. Noticed suddenly the 'Berkeley' was sinking, she had been hit by bombs. At that moment noticed a Messerschmitt flying towards us and diving. Fell on deck, hastily put helmet over head, and hoped for the best. Unfortunately, the Messerschmitt must have come straight for me, as, when it opened fire, I heard the bullets just below me in the side. Next second one had gone through my helmet, and I felt a bang in my head and neck, and another in my ankle, and thought the end of the world had come. Fortunately it hadn't. Messerschmitt was past."

By then, any further evacuation was impossible. The "Calpe" had closed to within nine cables of the beach where she came under machine-gun fire from German posts on the Dieppe breakwater. No sign of troops or landing craft, save derelicts, could be seen, and the "Calpe" returned to the cover of the smoke. The Naval Force Commander was engaged in signalling to the "Locust," which being of more shallow draft might possibly have been able to approach nearer, when Major-General Roberts received a last signal from the shore. It came from Brigadier Southam's Headquarters, saying he was compelled to surrender. The time was eight minutes past one.

"Air Co-operation Faultless"

The return to England was mostly uneventful, thanks to the Royal Air Force, for the cover maintained was still intense. Despite weather which had become overcast, the air battle went on with hardly-diminished fury, and the weary men on the ships, looking up, could see "Fierce fiery warriors fight upon the clouds in ranks and squadrons and right form of war."

During the voyage home, in addition to the general air cover provided, 86 additional patrols were put up to intercept specific attacks. By then, some of our pilots were engaged on their fourth and even their fifth sortie of the day. It was this devotion to duty, combined with the high degree of skill and training shown, which caused the Military Force Commander to signal to his Royal Air Force colleague, "Air co-operation faultless."

The expedition returned to the ports from which it sailed, some of the ships not berthing until past midnight.

In the words of the Prime Minister, speaking in the House of Commons on the 8th September, 1942, "The Dieppe Raid must be considered a reconnaissance in force. It was a hard, savage clash, such as is likely to become increasingly numerous as the war deepens. We had to get all the information necessary before landing operations on a much larger scale. This raid, apart from its reconnaissance value, brought about an extremely satisfactory air battle in the west, which Fighter Command wish they could repeat every week."

The results to which the Prime Minister referred were indeed of the highest importance. Two were outstanding. In the first place we learnt much about the German defences in the West. In the second place, and of still greater value, was the first-hand experience we acquired of the conditions which may be met with in a large-scale assault on a strongly-held Channel port. The details of these experiences must not be revealed. The enemy will know in due course how we have profited by them. While the Dieppe raid was an indispensable prelude for what was to take place later, in a sense it was also the culminating point in the series of reconnaissances of which some account has now been given. Certain of the results achieved became visible later when a combined operation on a much larger scale was successfully launched; others will appear in the major assaults to come.

These results were purchased at a high cost in casualties. The Canadians suffered particularly heavily. It was announced in Ottawa after the operation that of 5,000 Canadian troops engaged a total of 3,350 were killed, wounded or missing. Subsequent announcements raised the total to 3,372. This included 593 officers and other ranks killed or died of wounds, 1,901 who were prisoners of war or otherwise detained on the Continent, and 287 missing; while 591 returned wounded to England.

It is sometimes possible to judge the effect of action otherwise than by the public analysis of such of its results as the military authorities are able to divulge in time of war. Phrases like "synchronisation" and "timing" do not always convey the full importance which should be attached to them unless a yard-stick is provided by which they can be measured. Such a yard-stick was produced by Goebbels. It was the reactions of his propaganda machine.

The enemy was very badly rattled. For the better part of a day, Axis wireless stations broadcast statements which were at once fantastic and contradictory. Thus they said the raid showed every sign of hasty preparation; it had been ordered by the Prime Minister on his return from Moscow four days previously as a sop to Stalin. Almost in the same breath they said that it was the culmination of ten months' planning of so extensive a nature that the Chief of Combined Operations had paid a special visit to the United States of America in connection with its preparation. A little later they maintained that the raid was meant to be the opening of the second front, a little later still that it was not a second front at all but only a raid. By these and equally glaring contradictions did the enemy betray his troubled and uneasy spirit. The phrase "perfect synchronisation," which passed almost unnoticed or was taken for granted by the ordinary British or American citizen, had for the Germans a most precise and sinister significance. They realised that their enemies were able to stage with success a landing on a scale heavy enough to make a still larger combined operation a practical proposition. Where that larger landing would take place, and when, they did not know, but German political warfare, which from the beginning of the war had taken and maintained the offensive, began on the day of Dieppe to turn to the defensive.

The enemy's apprehension concerning a major assault was well founded. Eighty days later the occupation of French North Africa began.

19. "THIS MAJESTIC ENTERPRISE"

One night in October, 1942, Major-General (now Lieutenant-General) Clark, Brigadier-General Lemnitzer, Colonel Hamblen and Colonel Holmes of the United States Army and Captain Wright of the United States Navy went on board one of His Majesty's submarines which shortly afterwards put to sea. Accompanying them were Captain C. B. Courtney, Royal West Kent Regiment, Lieutenant R. P. Livingstone, Royal Ulster Rifles, and Lieutenant J. P. Foote, Dorsetshire Regiment, all three of them officers of a Special Service Brigade of the Combined Operations Command.

The mission on which the American officers were setting out was of great secrecy and importance, for they had been ordered to get into touch with a number of French officers and civilians living in French North Africa. These men were known to be devoted to the cause of the United Nations and to be ready with information which would have a great, perhaps a vital effect on the plans for an expedition far greater than any yet mounted in this war. It was the duty of the three British officers to put the Americans ashore at a chosen spot, protect them while they went about their business there, and take them off when it was concluded.

"We weighed," says Captain Courtney, "and put to sea about 2200 hours. . . . We continued on the surface throughout the next day at an average speed of some 12 knots. This risk was taken because the time factor was of the utmost importance; we had a long way to go and not very much time. During the morning of that day, General Clark called us into the wardroom and explained what he wanted us to do. He told me that certain persons desired high-ranking American officers to come secretly so that the plans might be concerted. General Clark then went on to explain that a white light would be shining from the particular point where we were to land. He and his staff were entirely in our 'good' hands and would not, therefore, interfere in any way except that certain political considerations must be borne in mind. In his words,

it was 'our baby.' That made things much easier. They were a grand
crowd to work with. Livingstone, Foote and I then made our plans."

The White Light Was Shining

During the voyage, the feat, by no means easy, of getting from the
deck of a submarine into a rubber boat was practised, and when this
palled the hours were passed playing bridge, and the American officers
were initiated into the mysteries of various card games popular with
the British Army.

Eventually the point chosen was reached and a bright light observed
burning on shore. About 2100 hours the party embarked in the rubber
boats, the American officers carrying their uniforms in haversacks and
wearing a strange collection of civilian clothes. All went well, except
that the last boat, with Captain Courtney alone in it, was upset and
damaged by striking one of the fore planes of the submarine. This delayed matters, but the others went on their way, soon hotly pursued by
Captain Courtney and Colonel Hamblen.

"While making for the shore, our ears were apprehensively cocked,
so to speak, for any further signs of leaks and I kept asking Colonel
Hamblen whether the seat of his trousers was becoming wet—or wetter.
I was forward and Colonel Hamblen aft and both of us paddling hard.
All this time, the light was still shining, which made navigation sim-
pler. We proceeded towards the shore at such a speed that we caught
up with the rest of the party before they beached. The Colonel discovered a number of new muscles on the way in."

Arrived on shore they were met by those they had come to seek.
"They led us up the path to the house, which was large, with white
walls and a red roof built round a big courtyard in the centre of which
was a small garden. It was two-storeyed and was in fact a well-to-do
colonial house. There were plenty of rooms and lots of beds. The furniture was ornate, of the 1900 vintage."

The three British officers passed the rest of the night in sleep, and
the following morning in cleaning their arms and repairing the boats.
During the day there were several alarms, but it was not until about
seven in the evening that anything serious occurred. At that hour a
message was received that two gendarmes were on their way from the
nearest police post to investigate movement round what was supposed
to be a deserted house. The mission and their hosts, who had been
deliberating for many hours, leapt into swift action.

"The alarm occurred just after supper, and I saw the French officers tearing off their uniforms and pulling on civilian trousers and coats, etc., but our party remained in uniform. The Frenchmen then thrust General Clark, his officers and the three of us down into a very dusty cellar just off the courtyard beneath a line of store rooms, and told us to keep absolutely quiet. The people upstairs spread dust and put tin cans over the trap door through which we had entered. The cellar was pitch dark and quite small, so that we were all pretty close together. We remained as motionless as we could, and soon heard people walking up and down in the courtyard outside, whistling in a nonchalant manner. There was a certain amount of discussion in whispers as to whether I should be sent down to the beach to contact the submarine with the wireless set. It was decided that it was better to wait and see what happened.

"How Do You Load This Goddam Thing?"

"All this time, the dust had been seeping through the roof of the cellar and got in my throat, and I had a great desire to cough. I lay on my stomach, thrust a handkerchief into my mouth and attempted to stifle the cough, without success. I felt a hand beating on my back and heard a voice which sounded like General Clark's say, 'Have some gum.' I removed the handkerchief and inserted the gum, which eventually did the trick. Shortly after this, we heard General Clark fiddling with his carbine. He said, 'How the hell do you load this goddam thing?' This remark was followed by unpleasant clicking noises from his direction. We asked him to put it away in case he pressed the wrong button. Then we heard knocking at the gates of the house and a voice in French say, 'Ouvrez.' After that, voices were heard carrying on a conversation in French which lasted for about ten minutes. The words could not be distinguished, but it was presumably our hosts parleying with the local gendarmerie. After a while we were let out of the cellar, having been there for about one and a half hours, and were told that the gendarmes had gone but were not satisfied, and that we must get away. We took the boats out of the house and hurried down to the beach."

The time was now about nine o'clock. The submarine was ready and waiting, and Captain Courtney spoke to her Commanding Officer, using a special code which they had invented.

"Our recognition signal was some incident known only to both of us. The No. 1 of the submarine had just received a photograph of his girl, and I mentioned that in my first signal and was answered by the submarine Commander, who capped my statement with the story of his reactions after receiving the photograph. This back-chat across the ether was very effective cover, for nobody could have understood it but our two selves. We decided that General Clark and Captain Livingstone should try to get through the surf first. They had got most of the way when a big comber came out of the darkness. We saw them paddling up the slope of the comber, and when they reached the top they looked almost as though they were hanging vertically. The bow of the boat reared up and they fell backwards underneath the boat. We salved General Clark and Captain Livingstone and a certain amount of the gear. Neither was hurt and the boat was fortunately undamaged.

"General Clark then decided that we should have to wait and try again later, when, it was hoped, the surf might have moderated. We concealed the boats once more in the bushes and posted sentries, working on a roster in which everyone but General Clark took part. Those not on duty returned to the house. As nearly as possible, each sentry remained on duty for one hour. I then contacted the submarine, told them we were in difficulties and asked her to go out to sea and wait our further call. General Clark was soaking wet, so General Lemnitzer lent him his trousers and shirt, and then did sentry-go beneath a bush in his underclothes. He managed to acquire some trousers from somewhere, but I am not quite sure who from. He made up the upper part of his clothing from Lieutenant Foote. I was unable to be of any sartorial assistance, for I was soaking wet too. After that we sat on the beach and watched the waves, counting them to see whether they were going down or not."

"A Windmill Going Out to Sea"

Further examination of the beach and the surf enabled Captain Courtney to find a spot where the waves were less violent and there was a chance that the boats might be successfully launched. The difficulty was that for the first 15 yards the water was shallow; then the beach suddenly shelved to a depth of four or five fathoms. After some discussion it was decided to make another attempt to reach the submarine, for every moment's delay rendered detection more likely, which would mean very grave consequences to their French hosts. Four of the Frenchmen stripped and launched each boat in turn through the heavy surf. The first to leave were General Clark and Captain Wright, who safely surmounted a huge comber. "We then saw something like a windmill going out to sea, much to our relief." General Lemnitzer and Lieutenant Foote in the next boat, and Captain Courtney and Colonel Hamblen in the third, were less fortunate. They were all upset by the waves. "We swam ashore, a medley of arms and legs. I had impressed upon the Colonel," says Captain Courtney, "that at all costs he must keep his paddle. At one moment all I saw was an arm holding it aloft from the surf like Excalibur from the mere." At the next attempt all got away safely, only just in time.

"As the submarine turned to the eastward, we saw two bright pairs of headlights rushing along the Route Nationale and, as we watched, they stopped at the house and did not go past. We learnt later that this was a full-dress raid by the local gendarmerie.

"I think the thing that we welcomed most when we got on board was the peculiar oily smell of the submarine, which was like rare perfume to us. Once inside, General Clark and General Lemnitzer slapped each other on the back, and we all had a good stiff tot of Navy rum. We then went to bed.

"Next day, we kept a rendezvous with a Catalina aircraft and transferred General Clark and his party with their baggage to the aircraft. The crew of the submarine asked permission of the Captain to come up on the casing and give General Clark and his party a good cheer, and this was done. We then submerged gratefully and proceeded back to Gib. arriving about 1000 hours, when the Commanding Officer of the submarine (Lieutenant Jewell) and I celebrated our birthdays."

The information thus obtained was of great value and was put to immediate use.

At eight o'clock in the morning of Thursday, the 5th November, 1942, Lieutenant-General Eisenhower of the United States Army and his Staff landed at Gibraltar. He had arrived to take supreme command of a combined operation greatly exceeding in magnitude and scope anything which had been attempted in modern war. He entered Headquarters specially prepared for him in the bowels of Gibraltar's Rock. They were proof against the heaviest bomb or shell and had been constructed in a few weeks. Here, in an atmosphere somewhat humid despite the air conditioning, the last touches were put to a most elaborate plan involving landings in force at eleven points in French North Africa, from Casablanca on the West to Algiers on the East.

Before dawn broke on 8th November, 1942, the assault landing craft, lowered from their parent ships, were moving towards the chosen beaches. At eleven minutes past two in the morning General Eisenhower learnt that successful landings had been made at Algiers and near Oran. At 6.38 a.m. General Patton, the American officer commanding the Western Task Force, reported that his attack on Casablanca had been initiated on schedule. From that moment action rose to a crescendo.

It is still in progress; this is neither the time nor the place to describe it. But we know that the long months of raiding the coasts of the enemy, of training more and yet more men in the art of amphibious warfare, were not in vain.

20. TO THE DAY OF ASSAULT

The first troops of this war to carry out a combined operation against the enemy were borne in eight motor boats. Those who went with the expedition to North Africa, with which this story closes, sailed in convoys numbering hundreds of ships. Such is the measure of the growth of Combined Operations in the past 30 months, and the end has not yet been reached—perhaps not even the end of the beginning.

It is seldom wise to dwell on achievements, especially in time of war when the future must always be of greater moment than the past. Yet the old truism that the future is a function of the past is never more apposite than when applied to combined operations. They can only be successfully conducted by trained men, sailors, soldiers and airmen; and the more experience those men acquire, the higher becomes the standard of their training.

Modern war has little use for amateurs; impatience and improvisation seldom win battles. It was dogged months of training under instructors who knew from experience what were the hazards and opportunities of attack which produced Alexander's phalanx, Cæsar's legions, Cromwell's Ironsides, French's "Old Contemptibles," Montgomery's Eighth Army. None know this better than those who engage in combined operations, for theirs is the hardest problem of war, and in this war it has become three-dimensional. Troops, even veterans, are useless unless the Navy can put them ashore at the chosen place and at the right time, and both may fail if there is no air cover above them.

It is the principal function of the Combined Operations Command to help to make it possible for the greatest number of trained officers and men to land successfully on the enemy's coasts and thereafter to destroy him. It is on the problem of the landing and the maintenance in the early stages of the force once landed that it is concentrating. To this end no energy, no effort is spared. Each operation, or, to put it another way, every experiment in attack, is most carefully planned by staff officers, many of whom subsequently take part in it. The report of every

Force Commander submitted after the conclusion of an operation contains a section on the lessons learnt. This is in accordance with an old and sound tradition, begun in the 18th century, for it must not be forgotten that the combined operations of this war are the direct descendants of the "conjunct expeditions" of the past.

"The bellows was forgot at Lorient . . . there was no planks for mounting a battery at Placentia . . . the smoke carried was just adequate . . . from the remaining boxes two detonators were missing . . . it is recommended that a stock of self-heating soup be carried . . . it is suggested that the possibility of fitting a gun turret abaft the engine room should be investigated . . ." Observations such as these, picked at random, are to be found in reports from 1759 to 1942. They show how meticulously every detail of an operation is recorded for future study.

The first steps to solve the problem of invading Europe were taken two and a half years ago, when a force to carry out raids on the enemy was raised; but raiding is not an end in itself, only the means to the ultimate end—invasion and occupation. These raids are, however, of great value. They may be described as the most essential part of the programme of training; but, apart from this aspect, their effect on the enemy must be considered. The fear they engender in the hearts of the Germans is to be measured by the severity of the treatment accorded by them to the prisoners taken. The Germans have always been poor psychologists.

"To Win Bright Honour"

These "Red Indian" raids, to use the contemptuous phrase by which Goebbels seeks to belittle them—though a closer acquaintance with the works of Fenimore Cooper might show him that Red Indians were stealthy, fierce and implacable—are keeping the German garrisons on the long stretch of occupied coasts in a state of nervous tension. At any moment "a steel hand" may reach out from the sea to pluck a sentry or the garrison of a lookout post into the night and the unknown. The raids compel the German High Command to disperse a considerable number of troops, badly needed elsewhere, along the western coasts of Europe; the morale of these troops is undermined, the will to resist of the enslaved peoples strengthened. Any raid may be the spearhead of an invasion or a diversion from the real point of attack. The enemy can never be quite sure.

The men who carry them out come from many formations, but the nucleus is to be found in the Combined Operations Command. Few in numbers to begin with, they are now a considerable force. This force includes the officers and ratings who man its great diversity of craft, ranging from the ocean-going landing ship to its pendent child, the landing craft. There are Naval Beach Commandos, Military Commandos, and Royal Marines. Most of the Allies have Commando troops. There are Royal Air Force Servicing Commandos, whose work on the airfields of Egypt and French North Africa is an earnest of what is to come. There are other Special Troops with special tasks whose exploits must, for the present, remain a secret. This is the force whose officers and men have trained, worked and fought side by side, and with many other formations and units, for the better part of three years. The value of the experience they have gained in the conduct of combined operations is hard to exaggerate. No large-scale attack on the continent of Europe could be successfully mounted without this experience.

Not only do they carry out raids, they also engage in larger operations —the assault on Dieppe is an example—with other formations of the United Kingdom, Dominion and Allied Armies, trained on the same lines as themselves at the Combined Training Centres.

The number of those in all Services who took, or are taking part in combined operations has steadily grown. Already six Victoria Crosses and 381 other decorations have been won by them and 481 officers and men of all three Services have been mentioned in despatches.

The tradition of combined operations, which began in the reign of Elizabeth, is rapidly reaching its fullest manifestation in the reign of George VI. Men of the Commandos still go out in the night-time with darkened faces,

"To win bright honour from the palefaced moon,"

but they are not alone. With them now is the great array of the United Nations, turned from defence towards attack. Their trained and gathered strength, of which the display in French North Africa was but a prelude, a dress rehearsal, is preparing for the day of the assault. When it dawns, the victory will be achieved by applying the principles learned in a long series of combined operations, of which that assault will be the last and greatest.